Multiculturalism and Diversity

Contemporary Social Issues

Contemporary Social Issues, a book series authored by leading experts in the field, focuses on psychological inquiry and research relevant to social issues facing individuals, groups, communities, and society at large. Each volume is written for scholars, students, practitioners, and policy-makers.

Series editor: Mark Snyder

Multiculturalism and Diversity: A Social Psychological Perspective
Bernice Lott

Multiculturalism and Diversity

A Social Psychological Perspective

Bernice Lott

WILEY-BLACKWELL

A John Wiley & Sons, Ltd., Publication

Blackwell Publishing was acquired by John Wiley & Sons in February 2007. Blackwell's publishing program has been merged with Wiley's global Scientific, Technical, and Medical business to form Wiley-Blackwell.

Registered Office
John Wiley & Sons Ltd, The Atrium, Southern Gate, Chichester, West Sussex, PO19 8SQ, United Kingdom

Editorial Offices
350 Main Street, Malden, MA 02148-5020, USA
9600 Garsington Road, Oxford, OX4 2DQ, UK
The Atrium, Southern Gate, Chichester, West Sussex, PO19 8SQ, UK

For details of our global editorial offices, for customer services, and for information about how to apply for permission to reuse the copyright material in this book please see our website at www.wiley.com/wiley-blackwell.

Library of Congress Cataloging-in-Publication Data

Lott, Bernice E.
 Multiculturalism and diversity : a social psychological perspective / Bernice Lott.
   p. cm.
 Includes bibliographical references and index.
   ISBN 978-1-4051-9066-4 (hardcover : alk. paper) – ISBN 978-1-4051-9065-7 (pbk. : alk. paper) 1. Multiculturalism. 2. Ethnopsychology. 3. Stereotypes (Social psychology) I. Title.
 HM1271.L53 2009
 305.8–dc22

                                                              2009008379

A catalogue record for this book is available from the British Library.

Set in 10.5/13pt Galliard by SPi Publisher Services, Pondicherry, India
Printed and bound in Malaysia by Vivar Printing Sdn Bhd

1 2010

To my grandchildren –

Samone, Adam, Ethan, Jason, and Ariel,

whose generations will hopefully take personal multicultural uniqueness

for granted.

Contents

1

Introduction

The Multicultural Person

Both the nature of what we take to be a self and its expression are inherently cultural (Bhatia & Stam, 2005, p. 419).

Each individual's many aspects are not fragmented and distanced from one another or hierarchically ordered on behalf of a ruling center but remain in full interconnectedness and communication (Sampson, 1985, p. 1209).

There are a great variety of categories to which we simultaneously belong ... Belonging to each one of the membership groups can be quite important, depending on the particular context ... the importance of one identity need not obliterate the importance of others (Sen, 2006, p. 19).

Each of us is a multicultural human being. This simple and basic proposition, most descriptive of those of us who live in contemporary heterogeneous societies, constitutes the basic (though complex) theme of this book. Within its pages the reader will find attempts to explain, illustrate and argue for the value of this assertion. A major stimulus for pursuit of this is the belief that the study and understanding of behavior, when guided by the premise of individual multiculturalism, will increase the authenticity of our knowledge and the reliability of our predictions. This, in turn, should enhance the relevance and efficacy of the applications of our work to significant life situations – in the interest of advancing human welfare.

Multicultural Psychology and Cross-Cultural Psychology

This book needs to be distinguished from those that are in the tradition of cross-cultural psychology or mainstream multicultural psychology. The latter, as defined by Mio, Barker-Hackett, and Tumambing (2006, p. 32) "is the systematic study of all aspects of human behavior as it occurs in settings where people of different backgrounds encounter one another." Multicultural psychologists prefer a salad bowl rather than a melting pot as metaphorical image, viewing the United States, for example, as a society in which groups maintain their distinctiveness (Moodley & Curling, 2006). They stress and argue for the necessary development of multicultural competence by psychologists and others. Such competence includes understanding of your own culture, respect for other cultures, and acquiring appropriate culturally sensitive interpersonal skills. To this end, professional guidelines have been proposed (and adopted) for education, training, and practice. Such guidelines are approved by the American Psychological Association (APA) for practice with persons of color (APA, 2003), practice with sexual minorities (APA, 2000), and practice with girls and women (APA, 2007).

The emphases in cross-cultural psychology are two-fold: first, to understand and appreciate the relationships among cultural factors and human functioning (Wallace, 2006); and second, to compare world cultures as well as subcultures within a single society. Cultures are compared on values, world-views, dominant practices, beliefs, and structures in order to recognize and acknowledge significant differences and similarities. The acknowledged ultimate aim is to uncover (or propose) "truly universal models of psychological processes and human behavior that can be applied to all people of all cultural backgrounds" (Matsumoto, 2001, p. 5). The focus is on cultural variability on such polarized dimensions as individualistic or collectivist perspectives, field dependence or independence, and on value orientations, ways of communicating, and so on, but the clearly articulated objective is to discover general laws of human behavior, or a truly universal psychology (Pedersen, 1999; Wallace, 2006). To accomplish this requires, as Matsumoto proposes, research with persons from a wide range of backgrounds, in appropriate settings, and the use of multiple methods of inquiry and analysis.

Both multicultural psychology and cross-cultural psychology have been of tremendous value in sensitizing us to the importance of culture in understanding human behavior and in promoting the necessity of cultural knowledge. The present thesis, elaborated in this book, is indebted to this work and to cultural anthropology but takes a different position and moves forward. As noted by Hong, Morris, Chiu and Benet-Martinez (2000, p. 709), "the methods and assumptions of cross-cultural psychology have not fostered the analysis of how individuals incorporate more than one culture."

Interpretive Lenses

I interpret issues of multiculturalism and diversity, as I do all other issues in psychology, through the lens of a learning theory oriented social psychology (Lott & Lott, 1985; Lott, 1994). Such a perspective emphasizes what people do in particular situations and assumes that all human behavior (beyond molecular physiological responses and innate reflex mechanisms) is learned. Behavior is broadly interpreted to include what persons do and what they say about their goals, feelings, perceptions, and memories; and explanation involves relating social behavior to its antecedents and consequences. Explanations must take into account the setting in which the behavior occurs. People and environments are viewed as mutually dependent and interactive, with situations serving to maximize certain possible outcomes while minimizing others (Reid, 2008). And, it is assumed that persons never stop learning the behaviors most relevant to their cultural memberships, and that these remain with differential strength in one's behavioral repertoire.

The approach to the particular questions to be dealt with in this work is further situated within the general framework of "critical theory." Such a framework can be described as a critical approach to the study of culture and personal identity that is informed by historical and social factors and an appreciation of their interaction (Boyarin & Boyarin, 1997). Fundamental to critical theory analyses are inquiries about the role of social structures and processes in maintaining inequities, as well as a commitment to studying strategies for change (McDowell & Fang, 2007). The related perspective of "critical psychology" (Fox & Prilleltensky, 1997; Prilleltensky & Fox, 1997) focuses specifically on issues of social justice, human welfare, context, and diversity. Such a focus demands that our research and inquiries cross disciplines, as will be the case in the material presented in this volume.

The intent of critical psychology is to challenge accepted propositions and interpretations of behavioral phenomena, and to examine the political and social implications of psychological research, theories, and practice. Critical psychology examines psychological phenomena and behavior in contexts that include references to power and societal inequalities, with the understanding that "power and interests affect our human experience" (Prilleltensky & Nelson, 2002, p. 5). This is a departure from much that is found in mainstream psychology where individuals tend to be examined as separate from their socio-political contexts (Bhatia & Stam, 2005), or as "cut off from the concrete materiality of everyday life" (Hook & Howarth, 2005, p. 509). In contrast, critical psychology accepts as a fundamental premise the intertwined relationship between persons and society (Nightingale & Neilands, 1997).

Within critical psychology there are some who perceive traditional empirical methods to be in opposition to its objectives (just as some in mainstream psychology see critical psychology as outside the bounds of good science). I agree with Jost and Jost (2007) that this approach is neither necessary nor helpful. They argue that "the goal to which contemporary critical psychologists *should aspire* ... [is to work] towards an accurate, empirically grounded scientific understanding" of the human situation (p. 299). In fact, it can be argued further that the best means of achieving a just society and social change is through the investigation and communication of empirically sound and verifiable relationships. There is no necessary incompatibility in social science between values and empiricism. All that is required of scientific objectivity is verifiability – that methods, data, and conclusions be repeatable and open to further investigation.

Persons and Communities

A major objective of this book is to examine the dimensions and politics of culture and how these shape individual lives. My arguments will be seen to have a special kinship with the position of Sampson (1989) who posited that the identity of individuals comes from the communities of which they are a part. Others, too, have appreciated the significance of these communities for understanding persons and their interactions with one another in multilayered social contexts (e.g., Shweder, 1990; Schachter, 2005; Vaughan, 2002). My approach to the communities of which persons are a part is to identify them as *cultures*, and my definition of culture, to which the next chapter is devoted, will be seen to be inclusive and to pertain to many human groups, large and small.

Such a position of broad inclusiveness has been judged by some to render the term multicultural "almost meaningless" (Lee & Richardson, 1991, p. 6), diluted and useless (Sue, Carter, Casaa, Fouad, Ivey, Jensen, et al. 1998). However, others (e.g., Pedersen, 1999), like myself, maintain that such an approach provides a more authentic understanding of how significant group memberships affect individual self-definition, experience, behavior, and social interaction. There are indications that the concept of multicultural is being redefined and widened in an effort to reduce "confusion and conflict within the multicultural movement" (Moodley & Curling, p. 324). Thus, for example, S. Sue (1994, p. 4) suggests that "Our notions of diversity should be broadened beyond ethnicity, gender, sexual orientation, and social class...Cultural diversity is part of the nature of human beings." Sue and Sue (2003) express support for an inclusive definition of multiculturalism and for the need to think in terms of diversity across multiple categories. Wide definitions of culture are being supported. Markus (2008, p. 653), for example, agrees that culture "refers to patterns of ideas and practices associated with any significant grouping, including gender, religion, social class, nation of origin, region of birth, birth cohort, or occupation."

Despite the perception of some (e.g., Flowers & Davidow, 2006) that multiculturalism has been a strong influence on contemporary psychology, there is still less than full agreement on its meaning. It was first launched as a theoretical, political, and educational perspective by the civil rights movement (Biale, Galchinsky, & Heschel, 1988). When introduced into psychology, it was clearly focused on cultures of race or ethnicity and emphasis was placed on the significance of this one aspect of human diversity. Part of the problem in dealing with the meaning of multicultural is a failure to clearly explicate what is understood by culture, a concept that has often been ignored or avoided within our discipline (Lonner, 1994; Reid, 1994). Another part of the problem is a reluctance to ascribe culture to a wide spectrum of groups, and a reluctance to equate multiculturalism with diversity.

My thesis, that each of us is a multicultural human being, includes recognition at the outset of the vital fact that not all groups or communities that constitute one's unique multicultural self are equal in their position in a given society. They may differ dramatically in power (i.e., access to resources), in their size and history, and in the magnitude of their contribution to a person's experiences. It is essential, as well, to recognize that in the U.S. there is an overriding national context in which Euro-Whiteness, maleness, heterosexuality, and middle-class status are presumed normative and culturally imperative. That there is a serious disconnect between such presumptions and the reality of life in the U.S. is illustrated by census data. With respect to ethnicity, for example, non-Whites now constitute a majority in almost one-third of the largest counties in the country (cf. Roberts, 2007), are 33 percent of the total U.S. population, and 43 percent of those under 20 (cf. Roberts, 2008b). But the presumption of Whiteness remains dominant, in support of status-quo power relationships.

This presumption is found across all geographic areas and all major institutions in U.S. society. It is reflected in university curricula in all fields including psychology (Flowers & Richardson, 1996). Gillborn (2006) asserts that unless a student is specifically enrolled in a course in ethnic or gender studies, higher education is still primarily directed by White people for the benefit of White people. Rewards are most likely to go to those who accept this state of affairs. Asante (1996, p. 22) cites historian Arthur Schlesinger, Jr. as maintaining that "anyone wanting to be an American must willingly conform." Asante likens this to being "clarencised (a word now used by some African American college students to refer to the process by which Supreme Court Justice Clarence Thomas is said to have abandoned his own history)" (p. 22). Others have written about the construction of normativity in which maleness and heterosexuality are taken for granted as points of departure for assessing "difference" (Hegarty & Pratto, 2004). This context of pressured conformity to the perceived norms for "American" provides the powerful "background" for recognition of the (multicultural) person as "figure."

Against this background, each of us is situated in a multicultural fabric that is unique. The groups or communities of which we are part and with which we identify, that contribute to our cultural selves, are not equal in power. Nor are they equal in terms of their salience and importance to individuals, or to the same individual over time or across situations. Acknowledging such complexity provides "multiple angles of vision" (Weber, 1998, p. 16). Such multiple angles/perspectives should encourage us, as individuals and as behavior scientists, to make more visible the experiences that pertain to our multiple group locations and their consequences.

This book is focused on contemporary life in the United States. It is likely that the multicultural nature of persons has been steadily increasing as a function of increases in the heterogeneous nature of our society, its institutions, roles, options, power inequities, inter-group contacts, and so on. Greater diversity in personal identity has also been attributed to the growth in globalization (e.g., Arnett, 2002), a phenomenon with widespread significance and consequences not just for national economies. Regardless of the nature of the precipitating historical and sociological changes and the number and variety of cultures that influence us, *behavior is best understood as a complex product of the cultures of which we are a part.* Our experiences and actions are thoroughly imbedded in a multicultural context.

A Proposed Social Psychological Perspective

That cultures differ is well recognized. What must also be acknowledged is that individuals in the same complex society, such as the one in the United States, are embodiments of such differences by virtue of their own unique multicultural selves. There are many intersecting cultures that define each of us as individual persons. Some are large – such as cultures of ethnicity, gender, social class, religion, sexual orientation, age, disability, and geographical location. Some are smaller – occupation, political affiliation, special talent, educational institution, unions, or clubs. Cultures differ in size and also in how they are related to (or constructed from) hierarchies of power, domination, and access to resources. Cultures differ significantly in their degree of *salience* and in the *intensity* of their influence, depending upon personal histories. *And for the same person, salience and intensity of a given cultural identity will vary with the situation, the time and the place, the historical moment, social demands, anticipated consequences, personal needs, and unknown other variables.* We will turn our attention to these issues in the chapters that follow.

As portions of this text were being written, presidential primary elections were being held across the United States. Writ large and possibly larger than ever before in the public arena was the multicultural personas of the two final Democratic hopefuls for the presidency. Senator Hillary Clinton is a White woman, with a politically powerful background and sets of experiences, who has always been economically privileged, and whose early years were spent growing up in a very White Chicago suburb. Senator Barack Obama is the son of a largely absent African father and a White mother from Kansas. He did not grow up in a middle-class household although he is now an affluent professional. He spent his teenage years in Hawaii. Both are heterosexual and Christian, both share the general values and aspirations of the same political party, both graduated from ivy-league law schools, but they have had different personal and career paths and different spheres of interaction. The diverse aspects of their multicultural selves will have different meaning and importance for them and also for those who heard and saw them and considered their merits for the job to which they were aspiring. It should not be surprising that there were White women who publicly supported the candidacy of Senator Obama (e.g., Maria Shriver, Caroline Kennedy), nor that some Black men initially supported Senator Clinton (e.g., Mayor Nutter of Philadelphia, and Mayor Dellums of Oakland, CA). Gender and ethnicity define powerful cultural influences but to neglect the importance of other cultural ties leads us to not understand (and be unable to predict) significant social behavior in multiple arenas.

Situating each individual in a unique and complex multicultural framework has significant positive consequences. As Pedersen (1997) noted, it helps us appreciate and emphasize that "all behavior is learned and displayed in a cultural context" and to be aware "of the thousands of 'culture teachers' accumulated in each of our lifetimes" (p. 221). In the next chapter, the concept of culture will be carefully examined. As noted by Matsumoto (2001, p. 3) "No topic is more compelling in contemporary psychology today than culture, and no other topic has the potential to revise in fundamental and profound ways almost everything we think we know about people." But we need to go beyond simply recognizing the contribution of culture to human behavior. We need to highlight and appreciate our individual multicultural nature. Doing so may help us to move beyond current tensions that pit "diversity" and "multiculturalism" against one another.

New perspectives more and more frequently include recognition of the significance of multiple individual identities (e.g., McDowell & Fang,

2007), the interdependence between individuals and their cultural contexts (e.g., Markus, 2008; Schachter, 2005), and the variations in cultural group salience across persons and situations (e.g, Sue & Sue, 2003). As noted by Pedersen (1999, p. xxi) "Each of us belongs to many different cultures at different times, in different environments, and in different roles." What I propose, however, is that we take this recognition several steps further. We need to fully appreciate the reality that *each of us belongs to many different cultures at the same time* – and recognize the consequences of this phenomenon for individual behavior and social life.

2

Culture

[I]ndividuals feel, think, and see things from the viewpoints of the groups in which they participate (Smith, 1991, p. 182).

[W]e cannot understand human diversity without understanding how culture contributes to the substantial variations we observe every day (Lonner, 1994, p. 241).

Culture is to human behavior as operating systems are to software, often invisible and unnoticed, yet playing an extremely important role in development and operation (Matsumoto, 2001, p. 3).

In the early years of psychology's development as a discipline separate from philosophy, during the last part of the19th century, there was interest in what was called "folk culture." But this interest waned as issues related to the concept were seen as too speculative and not readily amenable to empirical inquiry (Pepitone, 2000). Culture has re-emerged as a significant construct in the past few decades. In current psychological discourse, our definitions and conceptualizations of culture come primarily from cultural anthropology where culture is generally understood to refer to that part of our environment that is constructed by human beings to embody shared learning.

Definitions and Common Themes

An early definition, in 1891, presents culture as the incorporation of all socially acquired habits and knowledge (see Mio, Trimble, Arredondo, Cheatham & Sue, 1999). More than a century later, the core of this definition remains the same, despite multiple variations on the basic theme. Baldwin, Faulkner, Hecht, and Lindsley (2006) refer to the definition of culture as a "moving target" and devote an entire book to its discussion, providing an appendix of 300 variations. Nevertheless, for the purpose of the present text, I focus on what seems to be the essence of common agreement.

In this common agreement within social science, culture is understood to represent "socially transmitted beliefs, values, and practices ... [and] shared ideas and habits" (Latane, 1996, p. 13). Pepitone (2000) adds that the distinct patterns defining a culture are identified with by those who behave in accordance with them. Different aspects of culture are emphasized by others. Thus, Ray (2001, p. 3) notes that culture may designate what cannot be verbalized easily, "the unconscious cognitive and social reflexes which members of a community share." Lehman, Chiu & Schaller (2004) summarize the basic elements contained in just about every definition of culture – shared distinctive behavioral norms that are omnipresent and may appear natural, and are transmitted to new members of the culture. These norms provide interpretive perspectives that assist in the perception and cognition of events.

While some events are complex and some involve social interactions, an event can be as simple as "the smell of herbs and spices or distinctive foods cooking in restaurants and neighborhoods" (Forman & Giles, 2006, p. 98). Interpretation of what is smelled will vary with background, experience, and expectation. Culture refers to what we learn from others in the form of familiar associations or interpretations, beliefs, attitudes, and values. It prepares us to attend to some events and not to others, to ascribe particular meanings to what we experience, observe, and learn about from others.

In addition, a culture's interpretative perspectives may be communicated to those outside the culture in the form of artifacts or art or performances (West, 1993). Kitayama (2002) calls attention to the presence of cultural artifacts that may include tools, verbal and nonverbal symbols, and particular daily practices or routines. These are what outside observers use to learn about cultures not their own. When the new Museum of the American Indian first opened in Washington, DC, it gave space to a sample of tribes of varying size from all parts of the United States in which each could present to visitors what was considered to be the most representative of their history, practices, art, symbols, narratives, including the voices of tribe members.

Bond (2004) suggests that culture describes not just what persons within the group can or should do – "affordances" or prescriptions – but also what they should not do – "constraints" or proscriptions; and that it includes "a shared system of beliefs (what is true), values (what is important), expectations,... and behavior meanings ... developed by a group over time" (p. 62). To these can be added shared possibilities or encouragements, and shared adaptations to the particular circumstances of the group members (Lonner, 1994). Observed from the outside, a culture may be described in terms of distinctive food, dress, speech, music, rituals, texts, and so on. From the perspective of the individual within the culture, however, the affordances, constraints, expectations, possibilities, and patterns may not be overtly apparent or easily verbalized, since culture is lived, and only sometimes scrutinized or described by those who live it.

Culture is Part of Human Biology

It is culture that sets us apart from other animals and from our closest primate relatives. Culture is part of human biology (or human "nature") in that it is *made possible by our biological equipment*. It is the structure and function of particular parts of our biological equipment that provides us with the neural, skeletal, and physiological capacities to learn, practice, and adapt to changing conditions on a level not reached by other animals. As noted by Rogoff (2003, p. 63), humans are "biologically cultural." This essential and empirically accurate understanding is missed and obfuscated in discussions of culture that pit nature against nurture with arguments that rest on the false premise of separation between the two.

Contributing most especially to culture is our biological (neurological and anatomical) capacity for oral and written language that sets us apart from the most highly developed of other animals. A vital aspect of culture, therefore, is that it incorporates what is *both learned and shared* (Swartz, 2001). There can be no culture without transmission or teachability. Values, beliefs, normative behavior, and interpretations of experience are transmitted both explicitly and implicitly (or more indirectly) through the socialization process and through shared everyday life experiences and challenges (Lonner, 1994; Reid, 2002). Transmission is an essential feature of culture. What we attend to within a community, how we behave, what we believe, and what we anticipate must be communicated from one generation to another. This communication depends upon a common language or mode of expression.

Lonner and Hayes (2004) emphasize the pervasiveness of culture and the range of activities, events, and experiences that are shaped by it in every day life from birth through the rituals of death. The shared ways of behaving and believing are "created daily through interactions between individuals and their surroundings" (Segall, Lonner & Berry, 1998, p. 104). It is through social interactions that culture is maintained and persons are assisted in behaving in accord with prescribed and shared standards, values, ideas, and beliefs (Cohen, 1998; Swartz, 2001).

The most contemporary approaches to culture emphasize the active role of individuals as interpreters and modifiers as they interact with others and with their environments (Berry & Poortinga, 2006). Culture does not connote a static model of adherence to norms. There is always within-culture variation and change (Caulkins, 2001; Foley, 1997). A culture is dynamic, or a "work in progress" (Ray, 2001, p. 185), always in the process of developing and changing (Mullings, 1997). Contradictions and challenges exist and there are differences among those in the same shared culture. An important corollary is that no one learns everything that can be learned and people do not all learn the same things (Gatewood, 2001). Each person experiences different aspects of the same culture in a unique and individual way within predictable limits.

Diversity of Cultures

Some prefer to limit the concept of culture to what is learned, shared, and transmitted within large groups such as nationalities or ethnicities. This view was the dominant one within the earlier multicultural discourse in psychology but there are signs of change (e.g., Sue & Sue, 2003). The position I present in this work, like the one advocated by

Pedersen (1999, p. 3), is that culture be broadly defined "to include any and all potentially salient ethnographic, demographic, status, or affiliation identities." It follows that each cultural context in which we participate or behave will contribute to who we are, our beliefs about ourselves and others, how we interpret events, how we relate to and interact with others, and what we accomplish in promoting change in our lives and communities. Each of us will bring our complex and unique multicultural selves into our social interactions with others and into our interpretation of events.

When members of a group share a common history, or common locus in society, or common experiences, the fact of this sharing can shape a common identity. The view that culture reflects adaptations to "historical, political, economic, and social realities" (Mio et al., 1999, p. 83) is common to all definitions. Yet, within psychology some discussions of culture have been narrow and mostly limited to ethnic minorities. Others, however, have a broader perspective. As noted by Essed (1996, p. 57), for example, "The experiences of motherhood or a profession can appeal to a specific identity. We all have multiple identities.... We are defined by where we come from, but also by what we do." We are defined by the particular adaptations people in our group have made to their environments, as these adaptations and experiences have been shared and communicated across generations. The shared environments may be geographic or physical, economic or political, occupational or ideological.

It is meaningful and authentic, accurate and empirically demonstrable, to speak of "inner city culture" or Southern White culture, of military culture, ivy-league culture, women's culture, gay culture, Native American, or African American culture. Culture may be observed in a "religious enclave, an urban scene, an immigrant community, or a neighborhood" (Caulkins, 2001). By focusing only on what is distinctive or common among large cultural groups we neglect the vital recognition that "individuals incorporate more than one culture" (Hong, Morris, Chiu & Benet-Martinez, 2000).

The next chapter will focus on ethnicity and the factors that relate to past and present geography and nationality. Particular attention will be paid to the cultural significance of being part of a U.S. White majority or to a minority group. But culture is not the property only of groups that originate from the same part of the globe, or people who experience oppression or privilege, or who are socially marginal, or who may share physical characteristics like skin color. Learned prescriptions and constraints, and their transmission, also characterize those who share a political philosophy, an ideology, a religion, a profession or occupation or social status, a gender or social class.

Framing the discussions within this book is the proposition that behavior at a particular time and in a particular place is the outcome of the intersections of the cultures most salient to the person and most relevant to the situation. Consider, for example, what classroom behaviors might be similar and different between a working-class 30-year-old Italian American heterosexual male graduate student and an affluent 30-year-old gay African American graduate student studying psychology at the same elite university? What behaviors will be similar and different between a heterosexual Native American 40-year-old woman clinical psychologist and a 60-year-old bisexual Jewish American woman clinician in conversation with the same patient? And how differently or similarly will they respond to a 20-year-old and an elder within the same tribe, each of whom presents the same symptoms of depression?

Hong and her colleagues (2000, 2003) have introduced the concept of "frame switching" to refer to shifts an individual may make in interpreting events or issues from within the frames of different, multiple cultural identities. Their "dynamic constructivist" approach suggests that an individual can ascribe different meanings, even contradictory ones, to the same event, but that only one meaning will be dominant at a particular time and place, depending upon the other stimuli within a specific situation or upon immediately preceding events that have had a "priming" effect. I suggest that it may also be possible for several meanings of relatively equal strength to be evoked, reflecting the influence of more than one cultural background that may be relevant to the situation.

A culture is not the same as a "reference group." The latter can be defined as a group in which one chooses to participate or would like to participate; a group whose opinions or goals one values (Smith, 1991). We may use groups to which we belong or aspire to belong as reference points for behavior or beliefs, but cultural influence goes far beyond that. It shapes "who we are in spite of ourselves, effortlessly and inexorably as we ... internalize our community's habits of thought, values and forms of behavior" (Ray, 2001, p. 3). It is within our (various) cultures that we have practiced and learned how to behave, and what to believe and feel, in accord with prescriptions and proscriptions that were transmitted to us across time from significant others. Cultural influences continue to mold the specifics of development, beginning before birth, influencing subtle and also clear and obvious ways of doing things. Influences from non-familial cultural communities powerfully affect variations in adult behavior. Rogoff (2003) views cultures as "communities" or "groups of people who have some common and continuing organization, values, understanding, history, and practices" (p. 80). Such communities may vary in the extent to which the members are in continuing face-to-face contact or physical proximity and in the extent to which their influence is dependent on proximal contact among their members.

Empiricism and Social Constructions

Our cultural communities define us and provide contexts for behavior in particular situations. The relationships among these communities and the behavior of persons identified with them can be studied with multiple methods, and conclusions from such studies can be replicated and verified. The consequences of cultural membership for behavior can be direct or they can influence the relationships among other variables (Adamopoulos & Lonner, 2001). Thus, cultures can be viewed as both antecedent and dependent variables (Matsumoto, 2001; Forman & Giles, 2006). A review of relevant literature by Lehman et al. (2004) illustrates the conclusion that culture and psychological processes influence each other: "cultural paradigms influence the … thoughts and actions of individuals, which then influence the persistence and change of culture over time" (p. 703). And, as similarly noted by Rogoff (2003, p. 51), "people contribute to the creation of cultural processes and cultural processes contribute to the creation of people. Thus, individual and cultural processes are mutually constituting rather than defined separately from each other."

Culture, like all of our major social psychological concepts, is a social construction. This status, however, is not an impediment to empirical inquiry. I share Pepitone's (2000, p. 244) conviction that what is socially constructed can "be objectively real in the sense of having significant effects." We can identify cultures and investigate their antecedents, consequences, and role as mediators between variables. And it is imperative that we do so, since they help us to define and understand persons and make sense of human behavior.

3

Ethnicity

In the USA, the terminology of 'race' persists both in popular and academic discourse despite the acknowledgment that it conveys a notion of discrete, inherently different and permanent divisions of humankind which are not matched in reality (Fenton, 1999, p. 3).

Beginning in the nineteenth century, race has occupied an important place in the social science literature and, more recently, in the discourse on multiculturalism within psychology. But there is good reason to re-examine this concept and the literature in which it is embedded. I argue here that the concept of race, born out of the need to justify the oppression and enslavement of some groups of people by more powerful others, is now thoroughly discredited. Its scientific base has been found wanting and the concept has been abandoned by both anthropologists and geneticists. It is time for psychologists to do the same.

Ethnicity is a far more useful and definable concept, denoting diversity in terms of shared national origin and current allegiance. The frequently used "race/ethnicity" designation, which keeps one foot in the past, seems unnecessary. A more straightforward approach is to subject ethnicity to careful analysis and to consider its significance for community dynamics, sociopolitical issues, personal identity, and behavior.

Race and Racism

Discrimination against groups and individuals based on skin color and other assumed associated characteristics (phenotypic and genotypic) is the hallmark of *racism*. This construct can be operationalized and defined clearly by particular behaviors, beliefs, attitudes, and institutional practices that debase and oppress persons because of their assumed racial category (Clark, Anderson, Clark & Williams, 1999). Its reality, strength, and function in our society is well established. Racism is both an institutional and interpersonal phenomenon that includes negative attitudes (prejudice), beliefs (stereotypes) and acts of avoidance and distancing (discrimination) that can be overt or covert (Maluso, 1995). Its societal function is to maintain inequality by giving some groups more, and some groups less, access to goods and resources (Ossorio & Duster, 2005). This has been the case in the United States throughout our history, beginning with the occupation of land belonging to native peoples. Racism is implicated in all our "social ills, such as police brutality, poverty, illiteracy, disease, unemployment, crime, drugs, and urban crises" (Jalata, 2002, p. 107).

Racism is experienced in tangible and personal ways as avoidance, suspicion, poor service, harassment, and verbal epithets. It is "a daily fact of life" (National Advisory Mental Health Council, 1996, p. 102) in all areas and affects access to educational, employment, medical, neighborhood, governmental, and all other societal resources. It has direct negative consequences for personal and community health and welfare, amply documented by an enormous literature. When I first drafted this chapter, there was both open and quiet speculation about how seriously racist bias would affect the outcome of the 2008 presidential election and, despite the success of the Obama campaign, it may be some time before the answer will be fully known. We have witnessed, before and after the election, an increase in hate-filled and threatening messages. *But the facts of racism and its effects do not provide the concept of race with meaning nor justify continuing to use it in either scientific or popular discourse.*

Tied historically to the maintenance of racism, race has been an immensely significant sociopolitical category despite the fact that it is not reliably related to biological differences. It is, in fact, largely because race does not have a clear biological meaning that its utility for invoking, justifying, and maintaining status quo discrimination and oppression is so great. Races, so well accepted as real, continue to be presented in popular and political discourse without the necessity of scientific validation.

Early Usage

According to the American Anthropological Association (1997), our ideas about race are historically linked to folk taxonomies that followed the early explorations of America by Europeans who, for the first time, saw groups of people who looked different from themselves. In the 18th century,

> Carolus Linnaeus, the father of taxonomy and a European, described American Indians as not only possessing reddish skin, but also as choleric.... Africans were described as having black skin, flat noses and being phlegmatic, relaxed, indolent, negligent ... and governed by caprice. In contrast, Europeans were described as white, sanguine, muscular, gentle, acute, inventive, having long flowing hair, blue eyes,... and governed by law (p. 2).

Racial divisions of human populations were introduced into both scientific and popular discourse in the 18th and 19th centuries (Fenton, 1999; Smedley & Smedley, 2005). In 1925, W. E. B. DuBois noted that it was only after slavery was introduced into the New World that race became the prominent way to classify and judge human beings. He recognized that the concept of race was based on unfounded assumptions and pseudo-science, its main consequence being exclusion (cf. Gaines & Reed, 1995; cf. Keita, 2002). The historically identified races originally classified by Linnaeus in 1758 as African, Asian/ Mongoloid, Caucasian, and Indian were uncritically assumed to differ in skin color, in facial features, hair type, and other inherited physical characteristics. The idea of a Caucasian race came from the belief that the most perfect skulls could be found among people in the Caucasus Mountains (American Anthropological Association, 1997). To justify slavery and exploitation, some groups needed to be separately categorized and provided with distinct physical and human characteristics that could be ranked lower than those given to Whites or Europeans.

The main factor in making decisions about racial categories has been politics, not biology (Holmes, 2000). Race has been invoked to justify categorizations of "otherness" for groups of persons on bases other than skin color. Jews, for example, were designated by the Nazis as non-Aryan members of an alien race to justify their segregation, then persecution, and then destruction. But Jews were marked as racially different even prior to the Nazi era, and the tortured logic in this reasoning and the comparison of Jews to Blacks has been well documented (Boyarin & Boyarin, 1997; Gilman, 1991). Marking Jews as different involved "slipping within and among the categories of race, nation, religion, and culture … [and raising the question] Is a Jew white?" (Itzkovitz, 1997, p. 180). The new racial group that was created to encompass presumed Jewish difference (Pellegrini, 1997), and to justify their harassment and destruction, could be found discussed and described in medical and anthropological literature (Britzman, 1996).

Not only Jews, but also Italians and Irish and Poles were considered to be non-White races when they came in large numbers as immigrants to the United States in the late 19th and early 20th centuries (Biale, 1988; McDermott & Samson, 2005). These groups were labeled "racial" and described as "inherently and irredeemably distinct from the majority of the white population" (American Anthropological Association, 1997, p. 3). They were "widely viewed as filthy, diseased, verminous, intellectually inferior, criminal, and morally deficient" (Kaye/Kantrowitz, 2007, p. 11). In the 1890s, the Irish were said to be " 'Negroes turned inside out' while Negroes were 'smoked Irish' " (Patterson, 2000, p. 15). In 1899, a leading sociologist, William Ripley, classified Europeans into three races: Teutonics, said to be the most highly developed, were blond and blue-eyed; Alpines from northern Europe, stocky and chestnut-haired, came next; and then the least regarded were the dark Mediterraneans or Southern Europeans ("What's white," 2000).

Presumed Racial Differences

The most commonly invoked racial group difference is skin color. What is true about skin color, however, is that the skin cells of all human beings contain some melanin, the pigment primarily responsible for providing color. Skin color varies with geographical region and climate (*cline*), gradually darkening from northern to southern Europe and from northern Africa to central Africa (Fish, 1998). Differences are due to how much pigment one has and how it is distributed on the skin. The 6–10 pairs of genes that are believed to be responsible for skin color are not reliably related to the other approximately 30,000 gene pairs that are carried in human cells. In other words, "different traits do not cluster together in neat packages" (Cohen, 1998, p. 47). There are independent spatial distributions of hair type, hair color, blood group, eye color, head shape, and facial features. Skin color is not a reliable marker of race. Yet, as we know, it continues to be a marker of differences in privilege, between groups and within groups (Bell, 1997; Lilhadar, 1999).

The conclusion that there are no distinct human races is now widely accepted as a result of the failure to find patterns of genetic difference. Available knowledge tells us that human beings all had the same beginning as a species in Africa; and small groups then moved in different directions and different distances from their origin (Mio, Barker-Hackett & Tumambing, 2006). The more that anthropologists studied traits of human groups, the fewer significant differences were observed, leading to the conclusion that there are no distinct races (Ossorio & Duster, 2005). Within-group differences in the visible characteristics said to represent race are far greater than differences between groups, and "no matter how racial groups are defined, two people from the same racial group are about as different from each other as two people from any two different racial groups" (American Anthropological Association, 1997, p. 2). The genetic differences between groups and individuals cannot be sorted into discrete racial groups, and human beings are now regarded as a relatively homogenous species (Hubbard, 1994). Most human genes are also common to all other living creatures, with about 85 percent shared with dogs (Wilson, 2009).

Within a presumed "race," there are variations in skin color, blood groups, enzymes, and serum proteins (Betancourt & Lopez, 1993). For example, there is more DNA/genetic variation in a single African tribe than across all non-African peoples combined (see Boyd, 1996). Sickle cell anemia is found among some Southern Europeans as well as among Africans, but not in some tribes in South Africa ("Race" 1995). All of the blood types (A, B, and O) are found in all population groups (Zuckerman, 1990). Thus, "It is the culturally invented ideas and beliefs about these differences that constitute the meaning of race" (Smedley & Smedley, 2005, p. 20). One irony is that while Blacks across the world "have the most internal genetic variation ... they are most likely to be treated as if they were genetically homogenous ... [and] placed at the bottom of the social hierarchy" (Ossorio & Duster, 2005, p. 118). About 30 percent of White Americans have more than

10 percent non-European ancestry, and a Black person and a White person may have more DNA in common than two Blacks (Begley, 2004).

Brent Staples (2002), a *New York Times* African American columnist, has provided a personal example. He compared his skin color (medium brown) to that of two other Black men, Colin Powell, whose skin is a bit lighter, and Anatole Broyard, a now deceased *New York Times* reporter, who was dramatically lighter, looked White, and "passed" for White (Lee, 2008). Nearly all self-defined Black Americans have had White ancestors. Mixed ancestry is the rule in the United States, beginning with the importation of slaves in 1619.

Genetic testing provides evidence that the ancestries of persons considered Black as well as those considered White are complex and often unexpected. Brent Staples (2005) described his great surprise at learning that a little more than half of his genetic material was traceable to sub-Saharan Africa, while more than a quarter came from Europe, and one-fifth from Asia. Similarly, a program spearheaded by the historian Henry Louis Gates Jr. has given Morgan Freeman and Maya Angelou, for example, knowledge of White great-great-grandfathers (Lee, 2008).

Some recent medical research that focused on disease susceptibility and efficacy of drug treatments has seemed to suggest that differences between "racial" groups be reconsidered. What is correlated with certain diseases or reactions to certain drugs, however, is not race but specific genetic markers. Frank (2007, p. 1981) points to "the instability of ancestry estimates, the absence of established relationships between genetic variants and phenotypes, [and] strong correlations between ancestry estimates and unmeasured environmental exposures." There is a wide range of responses to drugs, such as ACE inhibitors and beta-blockers. Some drugs, in other words, that may not work well for African Americans, in general, may be very effective for a "significant percentage" of Black patients (Roylance, 2004).

Current Status

The conclusion that there is no biological reality to race, nor any packages of genetic differences that reliably distinguish groups of people, is now accepted among anthropologists and biologists. The earlier efforts within science to verify folk beliefs about human differences by examining bodies and measuring heads failed (Smedley & Smedley, 2005). Newly acquired evidence indicates that any two human beings are at least 99 percent genetically identical (see Harmon, 2007). Physical differences reflect the differing environments lived in by one's ancestors.

Beginning in the 1950s, statements by UNESCO began to challenge the validity of the concept of race and to suggest that its use was misleading and dangerous (see Yee, Fairchild, Wizman & Wyatt, 1993). Medical researchers know that self-reported race is not a reliable indicator of genetic make-up, and the National Institute of Medicine has urged investigators to no longer use traditional racial categories (see Schmid, 1999).

Despite the lack of biological reality, there are continued attempts to link race to differences in intelligence (e.g., Hernstein & Murray, 1994; Saletan, 2007). Following the historical tradition in which intelligence was measured with bumps on the skull or cranial capacity, the newer claims use IQ scores to posit the existence of significant, genetically based differences between Blacks and Whites in the United States. In rebutting such claims, Nisbett (2007) notes that approximately 25 percent of the genes of African Americans are the same as those of European Americans and that skin color is only weakly associated with IQ scores. He also cites a study that compared the children of German women (post-World War II) whose biological fathers were African American with those whose fathers were European American. The average IQ scores were the same. He summarizes additional data in a *New York Times* op ed piece aptly titled "All brains are the same color," and in a new book (Nisbett, 2009). The Flynn effect, described in detail by Gladwell (2007), refers to the fact that IQ scores around the world have been rising about three points each decade since their development, strongly suggesting a powerful environmental influence.

In the early 1980s, Yee (2006) introduced to the Council of Representatives of the American Psychological Association a Resolution on Race that was approved and adopted. This apparently long-forgotten Resolution "mandated APA to lobby the government to end the use of race and substitute ethnicity to classify the population" (p. 12). Others (e.g., Wang & Sue, 2005) now urge caution when using race as a variable or demographic category in psychological research. Helms, Jernigan & Mascher (2005) have urged research psychologists not to use racial categories as independent variables, since, lacking in conceptual meaning, they cannot be used to explain human behavior. Even more pointedly, the American Anthropological Association (1997) recommended to the Census Bureau that it eliminate the term "race" in favor of ethnicity or ethnic group. The Association argued that "race" has no biological justification and has been proven not to be a real natural phenomenon. Noting that 26 different racial terms have been used in the U.S. Census since 1900, including at one time Hindu and Mexican, the Association urged that racial classifications should be replaced by more accurate ways of representing diversity in the U.S. population.

Some important voices in psychology (e.g., Helms, 1994; J. M. Jones, 1991, 1998; Sun, 1995) who agree that the racial classification system is irrational and not based on science, have argued, nevertheless, that race (and racial identity) must continue to be among the phenomena we study as long as racism is a continuing sociopolitical phenomenon. It is argued that, as long as some groups of people share significant experiences of discrimination and oppression because of their socially designated racial categorization, race as a social category continues to matter and the concept continues to have a reality. But challenging and ending racism, and the realities of its tragic consequences for individuals and communities, is not aided by continued use of the term race, falsely denoting, as it does, groups of people presumed to share patterns of innate characteristics.

Those who suffer indignities and oppression fueled by racist prejudice and discrimination are not benefited from use by social scientists of a concept that disguises the real basis of that prejudice and discrimination – namely designation of inferior status by the more powerful in order to maintain unequal access to resources. I agree with Christensen (1997, p. 621): "Racism is about the unequal distribution of economic wealth and political power ... supported by numerous institutional practices and ... traditions." It is not about race.

Ethnicity

A new scholarly discourse on ethnicity stakes out a prominent place for it in providing a sense of who we are. These discussions are occurring at the same time as media and politics in the United States are reflecting a growing appreciation of ethnic identity, as its importance for individual lives and families is increasingly recognized (Worchel, 1999). There is wide interdisciplinary agreement that our ethnic location is crucial to, and a signal of, personal identity (American Anthropological Association, 1997; Fenton, 1999; Giroux, 1999; Markus, 2008). This location can result from the ascription of others, from birth, from individual choice, or from some combination of these.

What Does Ethnicity Mean?

Ethnic background denotes a national group from which one's parents/ancestors have come and with which one feels kinship and identification. Ethnicity represents what we have learned within our families about the traditions, practices, and customs of their communities of origin. Our ethnic group is associated with special experiences in language, music, history, literature, food, and celebrations that are similar to that of others of the same background. From ethnicity, one can derive a sense of shared and transmitted common heritage and values (Hall & Barongan, 2000). The basis of this commonality is national origin or what some refer to as our "roots" or common history (Worchel, 1999), the shared heritage of struggles and adaptations of parents, their parents, and ancestors. Taken from the Greek, *ethnos* means nation or tribe, and *ethnikos* means nationality (Betancourt & Lopez, 1993).

Members of the same ethnic group share a common history and set of influences and experiences, especially if they are also age cohorts. Members of ethnic groups learn about themselves not only from others within the same group but from the ways in which they are regarded or treated by mainstream institutions and by members of other groups. Ethnic experiences, then, may include, for some, various forms of oppression, discrimination, stereotyping, and prejudice, and for others, various forms of entitlement or privilege.

One need not live among others geographically to share in ethnic identification. This is true of immigrants (Deaux, 2006) – those who leave families to pursue personal advancement through education or occupation, or those who must leave for economic or political necessity and survival. What is important is that an individual "wants to be counted as a member" (Mio, Trimble, Arredondo, Cheatham & Sue, 1999, p. 108). How salient and important one's ethnicity is will vary across individuals and, for the same individual, will vary with time, situation, socio/political events, and immigrant or native-born status, among other variables. As Fenton (1999, p. 21) notes, "ethnicity as an element of individual consciousness and action varies in intensity and import depending on the context of action." The strength, significance, or salience of ethnic identity can vary for the same person at different times and in different contexts, and can vary among persons who may have similar backgrounds (Phinney, 1996). Multiple ethnic identities held simultaneously are possible and not uncommon (Biale, 1988; Hong, Morris, Chiu & Benet-Martinez, 2000; Root, 1996, 2001). As noted by Nagel (1994, p. 154) "Since ethnicity changes situationally, the individual carries a portfolio of ethnic identities that are more or less salient in various situations and vis-à-vis various audiences."

African Americans

We are accustomed to recognizing, studying, and thinking about prominent U.S. ethnic groups such as African Americans, Latinos, Asian Americans, and native American Indians but, in fact, each of these are categories made up of many distinct ethnicities. African Americans, who constitute 13 percent of the U.S. population – about 35.5 million (Aizenman, 2008), may have family ties to some particular region in Africa or the Caribbean or the West Indies. There is diversity among African Americans in skin color, ancestry, socioeconomic status, geographical region, and dialect (Caldwell-Colbert, Henderson-Daniel, & Dudley-Grant, 2003).

Common unifiers are the legacy of slavery, centuries of subordination and prejudice, and continued discrimination. Regardless of family origin, most older African Americans will recognize James Weldon Johnson's "Lift Ev'ry Voice and Sing" as the Black national anthem ("An anthem," 1999). Contributing heavily to a common ethnic bond or identity among Blacks in the United States is the wide array of experiences associated with racism (Nelson, 2008). Yet, particular components of African American culture will differ by region of the country, between rural and urban areas, and, of course, by social class. Consider, for example, such diverse Black ethnic communities as those in New Orleans or rural Mississippi and those in urban communities like Newark or Chicago. According to the U.S. Census, in 2000, 54 percent of

African Americans lived in the South, 8 percent in the West, 19 percent in the Northeast, and 19 percent in the Midwest (Hill, Murry, & Anderson, 2005).

What decades of research and personal experience make clear is that a major contributor to African American culture, regardless of gender, geographic region, or socioeconomic status, is systemized institutional and interpersonal prejudice and discrimination and their consequences for persons, families, communities, and the country as a whole. These ever-present ingredients within the majority European American society provide a contextual environment in which daily life and social problems are embedded (Maton, 2000). The continued practice of de facto segregation in neighborhoods and schools, and multiple societal barriers to achievement and power, are part of a collective experience that have profound and deep effects on African American culture (Steele, 1997; Wilson, 1998). It was only in 1969 that the last legal segregation policy in the United States was declared unconstitutional by the Supreme Court in *Loving v. Virginia*. A Virginia state law (in force since 1662) that prohibited marriage between persons of different "races" was challenged by a couple whose bedroom was broken into by a county sheriff and deputies five weeks after their marriage in 1958 in Washington, DC. They were arrested, ordered to pay court costs, and banished from Virginia (cf. Martini, 2008). Laws that prohibited "interracial" marriage had been enacted, at some time, in 40 states (Staples, 2008a).

Interactions with members of the majority culture, historically and currently, present cues of stigma, being less respected, less welcomed, less entitled, and less significant. An examination of the literature on teacher interactions with Black public school students (Chang & Demyan, 2007) found evidence of the pervasiveness of lower expectations, higher ratings of problem behavior, and more negative feedback. Entman and Rojecki (2000) analyzed images of Blacks in a broad range of contemporary media – TV network news, local TV news, TV ads, primetime TV entertainment, and Hollywood films. Their conclusion is sobering: "across the diversity of genres and outlets, the mass media convey impressions that Blacks and Whites occupy different moral universes" (p. 6). Negative images are still the norm and include Blacks as depersonalized victimizers. The "overall pattern" is that "although they do entertain us in songs and games – in what really counts, Blacks are takers and burdens on society" (p. 8). Even when the stereotyping is subtle, and even when African Americans are in roles of achievement, dignity, and affluence, Blacks are presented as distanced and excluded from White domains, with inter-ethnic intimacy or friendship a rarity.

A remarkable speech by Senator Barack Obama (2008), prior to the U.S. presidential election, in response to issues of race that emerged during the presidential primaries, directly addressed the real and powerful anger existing within the Black community as a consequence of injustice and racist discrimination. He spoke of the "brutal legacy of slavery and Jim Crow," of segregated and inferior schools, of legalized discrimination, and of color-based economic opportunities. On TV talk shows that followed the speech, prominent members of the Black community reinforced Obama's words. Despite the rhetoric of U.S. politicians during election years, the idea that we are all equal members of one nation is still more a hope than a reality. An almost unbelievable example comes from the convention of the Republican Party, one of the two major political parties in the United States, when it nominated its presidential candidate in September 2008. Of the 2,380 delegates, only 36 were Black ("Largely White," 2008). Another example, writ large during the 2008 presidential campaign, is the stream of both overt and disguised racist responses to Senator Obama in the electronic media and elsewhere (Landay, 2008). Staples (2008b) illustrated these with descriptions of Obama as "uppity," openly expressed by Georgia Congressman Westmoreland, and a reference to the Senator as "that boy" by Kentucky Congressman Davis. European Americans can only imagine the painful personal struggle by Senator Obama during the election campaign to avoid doing or saying anything that might evoke images of the angry Black man. Continued racist messages and frightening incidents have followed after the presidential election and been reported in the press (Associated Press, 2008; Knowles, 2008; Sullivan, 2008). Horrifyingly, many contain threats of assassination, and are reported from diverse areas of the country.

The cues and consequences of stigma are manifested in the everyday lives of African Americans in multiple ways, both indirect and direct. In 2006, a shocking 25 percent of Blacks were below the official federal poverty line (compared with 8 percent of Whites), and the median annual income of Blacks ($30,200) was two-thirds that of Whites (Swarns, 2008). To be African American in contemporary America is to know that more men of color are in penal institutions than in college, and to live in fear that one's sons, brothers, or partners will be among the former. The statistics are stark. In the United States, the average Black person is 447 percent more likely than the average White person to be in jail, and 521 percent more likely to die as a result of murder (Vedantam, 2008). One in nine Black men between the ages of 20 and 34 is in prison (compared with 1 in 30 nationwide). About one-third of Black men in their twenties are in the criminal justice system – on parole, probation, or incarcerated (Sue & Sue, 2003). There is also a huge difference in incarceration rate between Black and White women between the ages of 35 and 39 – one of every 100 Black women compared to one of every 355 White women (cf. Crary, 2008).

The Southern Poverty Law Center has identified a "school to prison pipeline" for Black children ("New project," 2007). U.S. Department of Education data reveal that African American public school children are suspended or expelled nearly three times as often as White children. Many of these children find their way into the juvenile justice system where they are four times more likely to be held than European American children, and others are admitted to state adult prisons where they account for 58 percent of the youth population. These phenomena are powerful aspects of someone's immediate day-to-day cultural environment influencing attitudes, values, beliefs, fears, coping strategies, aspirations, assumptions, and behavior.

To be an African American man (across social classes) is to have a lifespan that is five to seven years shorter than that of a European American man (Sue & Sue, 2003), an average life expectancy that is closer to men in Vietnam or El Salvador than it is to U.S. White men (Penner, Albrecht, Coleman, & Norton, 2007). Significant and large disparities in health care access and health outcomes are well known; they can be seen in infant mortality rate and in all major diseases and survival rates. This knowledge transcends "statistics" and is part of lived experience within the low-income Black community. According to van Ryn (cited in Penner et al. 2007), physicians' responses to a patient include the stereotypes activated by the patient's social category, influencing interpretation of symptoms, diagnosis, and treatment decisions. An empirical study by van Ryn and Burke found that, regardless of individual patient attributes, physicians reported their Black patients as likely to be less intelligent and educated than White patients, less likely to follow medical instructions, and more likely to abuse drugs. What does this state of affairs contribute to the anxieties, knowledge, expectations, and behavior that adults pass on to their children?

To be African American often means being perceived by European Americans as a potential threat or a probable thief. Carbado (2005) shares the personal strategies he employs to try to override this perception when he goes to a department store: "I might, for example, dress 'respectable' ... Purchasing an item, especially something expensive, immediately on entering the store is another strategy I can employ to disabuse people of my 'blackness'" (p. 193). He notes that White people (i.e., middle-class White people) are not required to take similar steps.

Gender intersects with ethnicity to produce special vulnerabilities and negative experiences for African American men. Dottolo and Stewart (2008) cite a 2004 study by Young that found that nearly all of an interviewed group of Black men, but none of the White men, reported having been detained by the police at some time. All of the men, interviewed in their fifties, had attended the same high school. Expectation of police harassment is common in African American communities, a salient issue especially for boys and men, but also for parents who need to prepare their children somehow for the realities of discrimination.

The personal toll taken by stereotyped beliefs about African Americans is highlighted by the literature on "stereotype threat" (Marx, Brow & Steele, 1999; Steele, 1997; Steele & Aronson, 1998). Such threat is described as situational and can be expected to occur when negative stereotypes about one's group can be used to interpret one's behavior. To experience stereotype threat, one need not believe that the stereotype is true of oneself but only fear that others will invoke it in the particular situation one is in. The research suggests that such threat is particularly damaging to African Americans who identify with academic or particular career domains.

Stereotype threat as well as other elements of the Black experience will have different consequences for different segments of the U.S. Black culture. Senator Obama has been chosen by the citizens of the United States to be the country's 44th President, thus reaching a place in U.S. politics and history beyond what anyone could have predicted or expected for an African American. Yet, publicly not in support of Obama's candidacy during the primary elections were some among the nation's most well-known former Civil Rights advocates, older Black men who have achieved considerable individual economic and political power (e.g., Ron Dellums, mayor of Oakland Ca; Andrew Young, former mayor of Atlanta, GA; and Rep. Rangel, Congressman from New York). For a time, the 42 members of the House Congressional Black Caucus was split in its support for Senator Obama, as were some of the best known Black clergymen and mayors (Bai, 2008). Rep. John Lewis of Georgia, originally among the group of non-supporters, later declared himself for Senator Obama after what he has described as a momentous conversation with himself. These men may be viewed as representatives of a culture within a culture; they share beliefs and behaviors that situate them in an older African American generation. As suggested by Nelson (2008, p. 19), they "tell us more about what has been than what lies ahead." Some younger members of the Congressional Black Caucus like Barbara Lee of California and Jesse Jackson, Jr. from Illinois were early supporters of Senator Obama. These newer generation emerging African American leaders may be more comfortable in the larger national community as a result of their education and post-civil rights-era experiences.

Some within the older generation have expressed the fear that Senator Obama's election will lead policy makers to the erroneous conclusion that racist prejudice and discrimination have abated, or been eradicated (cf. Swarns, 2008). While the situations are not comparable, these fears remind me of others. In the 1960s, I taught at a historically Black College where I met and worked among members of a similar culture within a culture – what Frazier (1957) called the Black Bourgeoisie. Among the faculty (all of whom were African American except for myself, and most of whom were men), I stood out as a White woman, and also for my political and social activist perspectives and my non-middle-class background. The other faculty, highly educated and economically secure academics, were anxious in the face of student-led sit-ins and public demands for civil rights equality and, for the most part, were not participants.

There are other cultures within a culture among African Americans; in the chapter on social class I will call attention to the very affluent. But another example is that of street-corner or street-life Black men, first carefully studied about 40 years ago by Liebow (1967) and described in a book entitled *Tally's Corner*. The location of that study was a neighborhood in Washington DC, one in sharp contrast to the neighborhoods more likely to be seen by tourists, diplomats, and members of Congress. A new study (Payne, 2008), situated in Harlem, New York City and Paterson, New Jersey, reveals that little seems to have changed for street-life Black men. Payne describes the communities of his study participants (ages 16–64) as "economically impoverished,... [with] high rates of unemployment, challenged school districts, arrest, police brutality, infant mortality, substance abuse, and dilapidated housing" (p. 3 f.). Street life, Payne suggests, enhances psychological and economic survival through friendship and bonding and positive community activities. It also includes a wide range of illegal ones. Payne's qualitative and quantitative data reveal a shared ideology of attitudes and beliefs, particularly about economic and educational opportunities.

"The streets" refer to settings that include street corners, vacant lots, pool halls, parks, public recreational areas, and drug houses where chronically unemployed Black youth and men hang out and interact and where they seek recognition and respect (Oliver, 2006). Unemployment among Black men is twice as high as among White men, and the former earn 62 cents for every dollar earned by the latter. Oliver discusses "the streets" as an intergenerational ghetto institution in which values and norms and male roles are transmitted from one generation of marginalized Black men to the next. Despite this, however, the culture of the streets seems to be one that Black males who are exposed to it are able, at some point, to leave behind.

Within African American culture are wide, diverse, and multiple sources of pride, resilience, creativity, humor, achievement, and strength. That I have paid more attention to the negative challenges stemming from racism should not be misinterpreted. The data found in social science literature (e.g., Thomas, 2004) as well as the content of memoirs, fiction, and biography offer innumerable and varied examples of the role played by African American ethnicity in shaping dreams, hopes, positive values, and accomplishments, and art, music, and literature. From such sources we learn also of the powerful role played by churches, Christian faith, and spirituality in ethnic heritage and daily life. From studies such as the African American Women's Voice Project, for example, we learn of the value placed on maintaining connection to Black heritage, as a way of dealing with racist and sexist challenges (Shorter-Gooden, 2004). From participant observer and participatory action research such as that by Ginwright (2007) and Guishard, Fine, Doyle, Jackson, Travis and Webb (2005) we learn how Black youth and their parents in community-based organizations function as problem solvers, political actors, and pursuers of social justice.

Latina/o Americans

This ethnic category, now the largest minority group in the United States, consists of almost 40 million people, or 15 percent of the population (Roberts, 2008a). Latina girls make up 15.2 percent of all the country's girls (Denner & Guzman, 2006). Latinas/os are heterogeneous in terms of country of origin as well as educational and socioeconomic status, food, music, accents, holiday rituals, and shades of skin (Betancourt & Fuentes, 2001; Navarro, 2003). They include distinct groups from every country in Central and South America as well as Puerto Rico, the Dominican Republic and Cuba. The largest group (67 percent) are Chicanas/os of Mexican descent (Lui, 2006).

For the most part, it is the Spanish language, as well as the experiences of exclusion and prejudice, that serve as unifiers within this diverse culture (Szulc, 1999). Many Latinas/os, descendants of indigenous peoples in the southern hemisphere, prefer not to be considered Hispanic, since this term denotes descendants of families from the Iberian peninsula in Europe (i.e., Spain and Portugal). It was White Spanish and Portuguese who came to the New World as conquerors and oppressors (Fears, 2003), and while Hispanic is a U.S. Census category, it is not what identifies Latina/o ethnicity. Morales (2002) has suggested an alternative identity: Spanglish. This, he argues is "what we speak, who we ... are, and how we act, and how we perceive the world" (p. 3). It connotes an intricate mix of ancestry and the heritage of Europeans, Africans, and indigenous peoples.

While Latina/o Americans are diverse and represented in every social class, education level, occupation, and all other domains, they are overrepresented among those with low income, the unemployed, and families living in substandard housing. Nearly 25 percent of families and over 40 percent of children live in families below the official poverty line (Langenkamp, 2005; Sue & Sue, 2003).

Negative stereotypes about Latina/o Americans permeate our media and mainstream culture. In films, advertising, television, and journalism, Latinas/os are either generally absent or negatively and stereotypically portrayed (Aparicio, 2003). The current climate in the United States is one in which European Americans are warned in the media about "the browning of America" (Ramos-Zayas, 2001). Negative stereotypes flourish, and fear and hate are expressed openly against undocumented immigrants who are subjected to harsh and unsympathetic treatment by those carrying out U.S. government policies. Most particularly impacted are immigrants from Mexico and Central America. As a consequence, open expression of Latina/o ethnicity has become problematic and personally dangerous in some areas of the United States. At the same time, ironically, Spanish is the second language in the U.S., and, in some cities and neighborhoods, it can be heard and seen everywhere in streets and shops along with other expressions of Latina/o ethnicity in food, music, and dress.

Nagel (1994) points out that, as is the case with other ethnicities, the situation and audience may influence public identification as Latina/o American. A Cuban American, for example, may identify as a Latina/o to non-Spanish-speaking others, or as a Cuban American to other Spanish speakers. In interacting with other Cuban Americans, identification may (or may not) be as a Marielito who came in boats through a special arrangement with the Cuban government in the 1980s; it was said at the time that Cuba thereby emptied its prisons and mental institutions.

The experience of Latinas/os, as with other ethnic groups, must be understood in the context of their history in the United States. Mexican American history includes colonization. As the young United States moved westward to the Pacific, White settlers were attracted to territories that were part of Mexico, and the original resident population of these areas became viewed as the trespassers. Ybarra (2003) recalls that his history books in Texas schools never mentioned the fact that Mexican people were in the state well before it became the 34th to join the Union. Little progress seems to have been made for Latina/o children in providing a respectful learning environment. Langenkamp (2005, p. 129) found evidence of a "reproduction of inequality" and an "undermining of students' cultural identity" in her study of a public school in Texas. Ybarra (2003) also recalls the movies he saw as a child in which the good White cowboy was pitted against dirty Mexican "bandidos." "To be Mexican-American," he writes (p. 27), "means that you live in a country where your ancestors lived but where you feel that you are no longer valued as a citizen."

The emphasis on negative challenges in the above text is far from a complete discussion of Latina/o American ethnicity. Once again, the reader is referred to a sizable literature of fiction and memoirs that celebrate strengths and values and ethnic pride (e.g., Alvarez, 1991, 2007; Chavez, 1994; Garcia, 1992).

Asian Americans

Americans of Asian descent, who constitute 5 percent of the U.S. population (Aizenman, 2008), also include very distinct and different ethnic groups varying in language, religion, customs, immigrant experiences, and sociopolitical history. They can be from China, Korea, or Japan (East Asia); Vietnam, Cambodia, Laos, or Thailand (Southeast Asia); India, Bangladesh, Pakistan, Sri Lanka, Nepal, Myanmar, or Butan (South Asia); or they can be Filipino (Okazaki & Hall, 2002). There are at least 60 separate Asian American groups, including native Hawaiians and Pacific Islanders (Austria, 2003). Up until the past several decades, literature on Asian American culture was scarce and Asian Americans were mostly an "invisible" minority (Sue & Wagner, 1973).

Today the term "model minority" has largely replaced older conceptions, presenting a popular image as stereotypic as the older ones. Research on teacher perceptions of Asian American school children, for example, reveals the dominant picture of cooperative, eager to please, academically competent, well-behaved, industrious, and reliable students (Chang & Demyan, 2007).

To counter the pressures of the civil rights movement and its calls for economic and social justice for minorities of color, Asian Americans, beginning in the mid-1960s, were presented in the media as successful and problem-free – diligent, valuing education, socially mobile, and earning high incomes. The actual picture is considerably different. Careful analyses show, for example, an enormous income gap between working-class immigrants living in urban ghettos (the "downtowners") and educated professionals and business owners (the "uptowners"). The economic profile for Asian Americans is bipolar, with Indians at the high end and Cambodians at the low end of the spectrum (Lui, 2006). The annual income of Asian Americans, considered together, is considerably less than that of European Americans with the same level of education. Yu (2006, p. 327) suggests that a visit to "the workplaces, such as Chinese buffet restaurants and Manhattan sweatshops, [will reveal] ... the everyday survival struggles of those less fortunate Asian workers" who do not fit the model-minority narrative.

A recent study of Chinese Americans (University of Maryland, 2008), who, at 25 percent, constitute the largest among the Asian

American groups, confirms their diversity. The investigators found a 50–50 split between the poorly educated and the better educated and more prosperous. The former tended to be more recent immigrants. But, the latter, despite their educations, were found to be confronting a glass ceiling, with those in the medical and legal professions earning considerably less than their European American colleagues. Academic success, the hallmark characteristic of the "model minority" is also far from an Asian American universal among all the constituent ethnic groups. A report by the College Board (cf. Lewin, 2008) notes that, as is true generally, Asian American SAT scores are correlated with parental education and income level. And more Asian Americans are enrolled in community colleges than in public or private four-year institutions.

Important in understanding contemporary Asian American culture/s is that each "began at the bottom of the economic and social ladder, and all faced intense racial prejudice and oppressive forms of social, political, and economic discrimination" (Endo, 1973, p. 283). In reviewing a novel by the contemporary Chinese American author Fae Ng, Mishan (2008) reminds us that while the first people not permitted to enter the United States legally were criminals and prostitutes, the next group was the Chinese.

In the 19th and the first half of the 20th centuries, Asian American immigrants, if not brought to the United States to work on railroads or mines, were unwelcome and legally excluded (Tien, 2000). In the 1800s, to compensate for the decline of slave labor, "Chinese men were recruited as cheap contract laborers to work in mining, construction, and to build the trans-continental railroad" (Austria, 2003, p. 64). Chinese immigrants who came to work in the California gold mines were described as depraved beasts of burden and opium addicts (Yu, 2006). The Chinese Exclusion Act of 1882 (not repealed until 1943) prohibited immigration and banned the naturalization of Chinese already in the United States. The Immigration Act of 1917 declared all people from Asia to be inadmissible, and the National Origins Act of 1924 instituted an immigration quota for all nations outside the western hemisphere. When China was our ally during World War II, a yearly quota was set of 105 Chinese; to circumvent this quota some resident Chinese invented fictitious "paper families" to bring others into the country (Mishan, 2008).

In 1952, immigration restrictions were liberalized but with very low quotas for Asian countries, and the popular media continued to present

Asian Americans as the insidious "yellow peril" – uncivilized, untrustworthy, treacherous, deceitful, and a threat to the American way of life (Yu, 2006).

Common to most older Asian American family members are memories of war, military control, suffering, and less than welcome entry into the United States (Chin, 2000b). A cyber exhibit documents the extraordinarily difficult challenges faced by Chinese Americans during their first hundred years in the United States (National Women's History Museum, 2008). Added to these is the unique chilling experience among Japanese Americans of having been imprisoned, many for up to four years, by the U.S. government following a presidential Executive Order in February of 1942. Two-thirds of those made to leave their homes were U.S. citizens.

The forced dislocation of families from what was called the military exclusion zone (states on the west coast) impacted those imprisoned as well as all other Japanese Americans. As recounted by former internees, many families were given only a few days' notice before having to move to an internment camp; they could take with them only what they could carry; and they "suffered not only the indignity of suspected disloyalty based solely on race, but also tremendous economic and personal losses" (Nagata, 2000, p. 50). In the camps, an entire family lived in a single barracks room; eating, toileting, and laundering were communal activities; and shortages were the norm. Some years ago, I saw such a room on display – a shame-evoking sight. When World War II was over and families moved back to the west coast, they faced discrimination in housing and jobs, and sometimes violence. The internment, many scholars believe, has been the pivotal experience for Japanese Americans in how they see themselves and their relations with other groups.

Each Asian American group has its own history, language/s, customs, beliefs, and relationship with the majority U.S. culture. Kakaiya (2000) has described aspects of the Indian immigrant experience. While the earliest Indian immigrants were male farm laborers, after 1965 there was considerable immigration of largely technically trained and educated professionals. More common, beginning in the 1980s, were Indian immigrants interested in business ventures such as motels, gas stations, and liquor stores.

Fiction and memoirs have added considerable qualitative information to what we know about Asian American life. Books by Jumpa

Lahiri (1999, 2003, 2008), for example, focus on Indian Americans whose lives are lived among others who are well educated and fairly affluent. She explores the close interrelationships among Indian immigrants of similar background and experience and poignantly examines the tensions between older-generation expectations and those of their children living in a new world. Highlighting the lives of Chinese Americans is the fiction of Maxine Hong Kingston (1976, 1980) and Amy Tan (1989). Their work reveals cultures in which the heritage of the past intersects with circumstances and issues of life in the United States. Readers are introduced to language, challenges, adaptations, beliefs, and aspirations that comprise the Asian American experience.

American Indians

As is true for other ethnic groups in the United States, there are cultures within cultures among Native American Indians. Among the almost 2.5 million people who identified as Native American or Alaskan native in the U.S. census of 2000 (cf. Sue & Sue, 2003), most relate closely to an ancestral tribe. It may surprise many to learn that there are about 600 tribal societies, each of which regards itself as a sovereign nation.

Among the Indian tribes are differences in language, customs, history, and size. There are tribes with only a few people living in isolated areas and others, like the Lakota-Dakota-Nakota or the Navajos, that are spread across several states (Peroff & Wildcat, 2002). The U.S. government provides federal recognition to more than 500 tribes; this entitles them to various services and their members to federal programs. The tribes that have not been officially recognized by the government do not have the right to legal and socio-political jurisdiction over their members (Cramer, 2006; Willis & Bigfoot, 2003). Federally recognized American Indian tribes constitute the largest landholders in the U.S. but their land and natural resources are held in trust by the government and managed by the Bureau of Indian Affairs (Lui, 2006).

In 1988, a Congressional Act made casino gambling possible in Indian lands, and 354 such establishments can now be found in 28 states, operated by 224 tribes. The Mashantucket Pequot's *Foxwoods* (in Connecticut) is the largest resort casino in the world. In addition to providing employment, its revenues are used for higher education costs for any member of the tribe and for housing (Cramer, 2006). Where such gaming revenues are absent, unemployment (for both urban and reservation Indians) is over 50 percent, and life expectancy is 6–10 years less than that for other Americans. Compared with other ethnic groups in the U.S., Native Americans have the highest rates of diabetes, tuberculosis, alcoholism, and suicide (Gray, 2002). The average income is 62 percent of the U.S. average (Sue & Sue, 2003). The economic and environmental exploitation, that began centuries ago, continues. Within the Navajo Nation, for example, many years of uranium mining have left behind disastrous physical devastation, abandoned mine sites, and probable radiation effects seen in high levels of cancer ("The cold war," 2008).

As the first people in what was to become the United States, American Indians, who originally numbered about 5 million (Willis & Bigfoot, 2003), have a unique history as victims of White settler expansion. The consequences of this for Native Americans has been loss of survival resources, traditional ways of life, and land, together with war, disease, broken treaties, and genocide. This history of forced colonization, fueled by greed and racism (Cramer, 2006), remains part of American Indian identity. Legends, family narratives, and tribal education provide examples of systematic efforts to undermine the survival of a people.

It was U.S. government policy that American Indian children be sent to boarding schools, often far from their families. They were not allowed to speak their own language, their hair was cut, and they were taught domestic or other skills. A character in a novel by Louise Erdrich (2005, p. 251) recalls an incident at his boarding school:

> It was forbidden to speak what the teachers called Indian; sometimes those words seemed to inflame a special wrath from the teachers.... One day, Seraphine forgot or rebelled and began to speak her own language and would not stop. The matron was showing girls how to mend cushions and chairs. In her hand there was a thick needle.... She turned and struck Seraphine. The needle ripped across the girl's face ... the scar of speaking her language remained across her lips all of her life.

While the federal policy of mandated boarding schools has been abolished, reservation parents now face a choice between having their children remain in poorly funded reservation schools or attending public schools off the reservation in nearby towns. Johnson (2008) reports on such a dilemma faced by Crow Indians near Hardin, Montana. The Hardin high school is growing (and was 70 percent Indian in 2000) while the Lodge Grass high school on the reservation is shrinking in enrollment. What Indian students can get at the town school are advanced courses in math, English, and the sciences, as well as the Crow language (in addition to French and Spanish), and Indian pottery making. At the same time, "[t]here is an unofficial line in the school parking lot, one side for Whites, the other for Crow" (par. 5).

Negative stereotypes of the American Indian and anti-tribal attitudes have remained strong in places where there is a significant Indian population and have re-emerged as a backlash to Indian casino successes. In addition, the dominant perception of lazy and drunken Indians has led to arguments that affluent and successful Indians can't be genuine or "real." The Indian man is supposed to be silent and illiterate, a noble warrior on the plains or a city street corner bum; an Indian woman is seen as chaste or hypersexual, with long braids and feathers (Cramer, 2006). A newer, contrasting picture is of spiritual and noble environmentalists (Hamill, 2003). From fiction by Tony Hillerman, for example (in too many books to cite), readers can get a more realistic sense of what contemporary life is like for Southwest Indians – particularly the Navajo, Hopi, and Zuni. Books by Louise Erdrich (e.g., 1984, 1986, 2005) provide insights into the lives of Plains Indians (especially Ojibwe). How little non-Indians know about the first people on our continent was sharply brought home to me during an exchange I had with a craftswoman during a Schimutzin celebration in Connecticut. At these yearly celebrations, tribes from all over North America compete for prizes in drumming, singing, and dancing, and vendors sell Indian art and crafts. I noticed that Turtle Island was indicated as the place where some work was produced and naively asked, "Where is Turtle Island?" It is what Indians have called North America, I was told, for over the past 600 or so years.

As a result of marriage with escaped and freed slaves, some Native Americans identify closely with African Americans. This is true, for example, of the Narragansetts of Rhode Island and the Seminoles of Oklahoma (Staples, 2002b). While the number of people who identify as American Indian has been increasing, it is estimated that the percent who are "full-blooded" is only about 34 percent, prompting questions about "true" identities (Foster, 1997). The U.S. government has used the biological criterion of "blood" to determine who is an Indian, and issues a CDIB (Certified Degree of Indian Blood) certificate to specify amount of Indianness. Tied to the CDIB is eligibility for federal programs, such as health care. The federal government is bound by treaties to provide federally funded health care for Native Americans, although it currently spends less to fulfill this obligation than it does for prisoners or recipients of Medicaid (cf. Miller, 2007).

The measure used by the federal government to determine who is a "real" Indian is in opposition to a prevalent Indian view that self-identification should rest on ties of kinship and relationship to the community (Jennings, 2008). Prior to contact with Whites, tribal membership did not rely on "blood" but on kinship through marriage or adoption, and some tribes continue to maintain their emphasis on ancestry, not considering blood quantum in making judgments about membership (Hamill, 2003). Peroff and Wildcat (2002) distinguish between "spatially" defined Indians whose identity in a tribal system begins at birth and "aspatial" Indians who may not be physically a part of a community but identify with it, with most Native Americans falling somewhere along this continuum. Fiction by any American Indian writer presents many examples of families and friends moving back and forth between city and reservation, visiting, staying, and moving on. Despite some fears that "wannabe" Indians are trying to gain tribal acceptance for illegitimate reasons, a casino-rich tribe like the Pequots had only 550 members in 2000, an increase from the 20 in 1983 (Cramer, 2006), but hardly an overwhelming one.

Friedman (1995) notes the importance of the point of reference in claiming an Indian ethnic identity. He uses two writers, Leslie Marmon Silko and Paula Gunn, as examples. In relation to White people, they are women of color. "In relation to women of color, they are Native American. In relation to Native Americans, they are members of the Laguna Pueblo" (p. 17). Other points of reference are the sites of interactions. Nagel (1994) notes that the same person might refer to her/himself as a "mixed blood" on the reservation, as a Pine Ridge Indian when speaking to someone from a different reservation, as a Sioux or Lakota when filling out U.S. government forms, or as a Native American when speaking with a non-Indian.

Jewish Americans

Jews constitute only $\frac{1}{3}$ of 1 percent of the world's population (compared to 33 percent who are Christian) and less than 2.5 percent of the population of the U.S. (compared to 95 percent who are Christian). But, despite the objective reality of their minority status, Jews are seldom included as a minority group in discussions of multiculturalism.

For centuries, Jews have had to cope with various manifestations of anti-Semitism and its personal, political, and economic consequences. Even in most of the early American colonies, citizenship was tied to Christianity; by 1800 "Jews could vote and hold political office everywhere except in Maryland and new Hampshire" (Lui, 2006, p. 246). In many parts of the world, Jewish communities have, at various times, been physically attacked and brutalized. A fictionalized description by A. Bloom (2007), for example, illustrates the horror and destruction experienced during an eastern European *pogrom* in the early 1920s. This is part of the personal story brought to the United States by countless numbers of Jewish immigrants. Such incidents preceded the Nazi-era Holocaust which, in one way or another, affected all Jewish American families, either through direct family ties or general emotional kinship. Another part of the Jewish American story is overt and covert anti-Semitism that, up until the 1950s, presented educational and occupational barriers and challenges to many.

Being Jewish provides another interesting example of ethnic complexity. A Jewish cultural identity can refer to one's religious beliefs or to a secular non-religious recognition of shared history, customs, language, literature, and values. Whether religion is acknowledged and practiced or whether it is the music, food, customs, and/or guiding life principles that matter most, "Jews experience themselves as members of a minority culture" (Langman, 1995, p. 223) – as "insiders who are outsiders and outsiders who are insiders" (Biale, Galchinsky & Heschel, 1988, p. 5). A common thread in Jewish values is *tikkun olam*, a concept referring to "healing the world", and a commitment to principles of social justice and progress (Feinstein, 2004; Siegel & Cole, 1997) – not always practiced, but held as an ideal.

The approximately 5.3 million Jews within the U.S. tend to be better educated and more affluent than other groups. Reliable data indicate that among Jews there are three times as many persons with postgraduate degrees as the national average (35 percent versus 11 percent) and that 46 percent live in households with family incomes equal to or larger than $100,000, compared with a national average of 18 percent (cf. Zuckerman, 2008). But Jews are found also among working-class, low-income and low-advantaged groups.

Within the Jewish community, there is considerable diversity depending upon the part of the world from which they have come. For example, Eastern or Central European Jews are Ashkenazi; Jews from Spain and middle-eastern countries are Sephardic. Among religious Jews, there are divisions and different sects and variations in degree of orthodoxy. Diversity is seen also among communities in different parts of the country. Kaye/Kantrowitz (2007, p. ix), for example, writes about growing up "in the Jewish land of Brooklyn" where being Jewish had to do with eating "cabbage soup and kasha varnishkes." And, on the far southwest side of Chicago can be found the Beth Shalom B'nai Zaken Ethiopian Hebrew Congregation that is led by an African American rabbi. "[W]hile services include prayers and biblical passages in Hebrew, the worshipers sometimes break into song, swaying back and forth like a gospel choir" (Koppel, 2008, paragraph 2). After 25 years of photographing Jews in more than 40 countries in all parts of the world, Frederic Brenner rejected the notion that there is an authentic Jew. He found differences everywhere, including between cities and communities in Israel (Goodstein, 2003).

Adding to the complex picture is the relative ease with which some Jews can "pass" as non-Jewish Whites, and avoid the stigma of Jewishness (Langman, 1995), by changing such stereotypic (and unreliable) ethnic "give-aways" as a last name, the shape of one's nose, or the color and texture of one's hair. In various places and historical periods, anti-Semitism and oppression forced the conversion of Jews to Christianity. These Crypto Jews found ways to hide their rituals and ancestry (Gitlitz, 1996). Disclosures of having been born into Jewish families sometimes come as a surprise, as occurred when former Secretary of State Madeleine Albright (reared as a Catholic) learned that her parents had been Jewish and that two of her grandparents may have been murdered in Auschwitz ("Albright concludes," 1995). The novelist Joyce Carol Oates revealed a similar recent discovery of Jewish heritage – a discovery that influenced her writing of *The Gravedigger's Daughter* (Oates, 2007).

European Americans

To be European American is typically equated with being White
(a term used by the U.S. Census). From an ethnic perspective, this can
mean associating oneself with, or taking for granted, dominance and
privilege and having little or no knowledge or interest in one's ancestry. While those who are White seldom consider whiteness to be their
ethnic identity, Hurtado and Stewart (1997) note that "people of color
are experts about whiteness" (p. 308), and see the connection between
an array of privileges and opportunities and being White (McDermott &
Samson, 2005).

The question of just who is White and the meaning of whiteness has
shifted with historical events. For example, the nation's first Immigration
Act, passed during the second session of the first Congress in March
1790, gave the privilege of naturalization only to free White person
aliens, and "well into the 20th century persons of various ethnicities
and hues sued for the purpose of proving themselves white" ("What's
White," 2000, p. 64). Until the immigration laws enacted in 1965, it
was White European ancestry that was the principal basis for admission
into the United States (Sachs, 2001).

For many European Americans, their whiteness is invisible and taken
for granted as the norm (Gillborn, 2006). Implicit in this is denial of
the role played by whiteness in the domination of those who are
deemed non-White and the sociocultural and economic privileges
associated with whiteness (McLaren, 1999). The assumption that
whiteness is a natural identity and that only "others" have ethnicity has
been identified with racism (Friedman, 1995), or domination and
supremacy (Gillborn, 2006). When White persons assert that they have
no ethnicity, this may be an exercise in power; it suggests that such a
state of being is just human, is to be preferred, and represents progress
(Perry, 2001).

There is extensive evidence that whiteness is associated with higher
status, privilege, power, advantage, and beliefs about merit. McIntosh
(1988) has identified 50 privileges (unearned assets) that accompany
being perceived as White, including the option of not being seen. To
Owen (2007, p. 206), whiteness connotes particular properties including: "a location of economic, political, social and cultural advantage
relative to those locations defined by non-whiteness"; being perceived

"as natural, normal or mainstream"; and being "largely invisible to whites and yet highly visible to non-whites." Reitman (2006) conducted in-depth interviews with a sample of male employees in Seattle's hi-tech software industry and found evidence of a "whitewashed" workplace, despite employees who were not White. The everyday practices and expectations revealed an assumption of the normalcy of whiteness.

White dominance and privilege is more likely to be taken for granted if one is Anglo Saxon than if one's parents have transmitted customs, beliefs, history, narratives, foods, or music from particular regions of Europe – for example Norway or Poland, Greece or Italy, and so on. Such ethnic influences are often revealed in novels (e.g. Krikorian, 2003, by an Armenian American) or memoirs. From such literature we learn about the Irish experience, the Italian experience, or the Greek experience, for example, and the consequences of growing up with these ethnic identities in U.S. communities. Howard (1999) writes about a new way of being White by exploring his Celtic heritage and making the connection to his ethnic roots and history.

A recent trend in research on whiteness recognizes its complexity and that its "meaning is imported by the particular context in which white actors are located" (McDermott & Samson, 2005, p. 249). Thus, Whites who are marginalized as a result of poverty or minority sexual orientation are not as likely to receive the benefits of white-skin privilege as middle-class and heterosexual Whites. These gradations in privilege are often apparent to, and understood by, people of color. Ramos-Zayas (2001) studied a mainly Puerto Rican neighborhood in Chicago and found that Jews in the community were seen as "not quite White"; that Poles and Italians were perceived as not cultureless, like other Whites, but as marking their ethnicity with festivals, food, and music; and that "hillie-billies" were regarded as the lowest echelon in the ladder of Whiteness" (p. 368) who did not share the power or privilege of other Whites.

Ethnicity Matters

The reader will have noticed that attention has been paid in the previous sections to those ethnic groups in the United States that receive the most popular and scientific "press." One striking and serious omission is Muslim ethnicity. It is hoped and thought likely that we will begin to learn more and more about Muslim life in the United States. Phinney (1996) suggests that there are three aspects of ethnicity that account for its psychological importance: distinctive values and attitudes; sense of belonging to the group; and experiences of powerlessness and prejudice associated with minority status (or the reverse). These aspects and others influence behavior in complex ways.

Beliefs associated with our ethnicity are implicated in vast areas of behavior and everyday life. For example, there are ethnic consequences for the shaping of views about the nature of illness, its treatment, and duration. Thus, the World Health Organization (WHO) has reported (cf. Watters 2007) that not only do ethnic cultures differ in the likelihood of using different diagnoses, but that there are different outcomes for patients similarly diagnosed. Patients diagnosed with schizophrenia, for example, do better in developing countries than in North America and Europe. Barber (2008) suggests that this is because those who are ill in cultures in the former societies typically get more support from their families and communities and are less likely to be stigmatized and excluded. The WHO is recommending that mental health work in disaster areas focus on support, and resist imposing assumptions about symptoms and treatment. With respect to post-traumatic stress disorder (PTSD), for example, it has been reported from Sri Lanka following the tsunami, as well as from Guatemala, Bosnia, and Afghanistan, that many of the most significant consequences to individuals exposed to the traumas of natural disaster or war are "not on the PTSD checklists" (Watters, 2007, p. 15). Differences among peoples are found in symptoms as well as in beliefs about the best ways to heal. Belief in the positive effects of discussing stress-provoking experiences is not a universal belief.

A 1992 study by Lopez and his colleagues (cited by Betancourt & Lopez, 1993) compared Mexican Americans living in Los Angeles with Anglo Americans in the same city, and they found important differences in reports of psychological distress and symptoms. In still another example, Arguello (cited by Landrine, 1995) found, among a sample of young unmarried Latinas, that anal heterosexual intercourse was considered a way to maintain their virginity and avoid the use of condoms (associated with birth control). Losing one's virginity before marriage would bring shame on their families and was a more salient negative consequence than the possibility of HIV infection.

Language can be a powerful ethnic cue. A sample of bilingual Chinese students in Canada were randomly assigned to write anonymous and confidential self-statements in either Chinese or English. Those writing in Chinese were found to make more collective self-statements and to show more agreement with Chinese cultural views (Ross, Xun & Wilson, 2002). The researchers concluded that those writing in English wrote self-descriptions that were closer to those written by Euro-Canadians. Similarly, Hong and colleagues (2000) used Chinese and U.S. national symbols as primes for a sample of westernized Chinese students living in Hong Kong, exposing some to such U.S. iconic symbols as an American flag and Superman, and exposing others to the Chinese symbols of a dragon and the Great Wall. On presumably unrelated tasks, the participants were then found to behave in ethnically predicted ways in making attributions, for example, about a pictured fish that was swimming in front of a group of fish: was it leading the group or being chased? Available to bi-ethnic individuals, the researchers demonstrated, is knowledge from either culture that can guide an individual's construction of meaning or interpretation, depending upon which cues are present and dominant.

Studying ethnic groups leads to a recognition and respect for diversity, while also sometimes demonstrating areas of similarity in basic values and/or ways of behaving. Schwartz & Bardi (2001), for example, reported similarities in some desirable goals and guiding life principles among large samples from many countries across the globe.

The study of ethnic groups has often focused on negative attitudes (prejudice) and discrimination directed toward minority groups, and on descriptions and consequences of stereotypes held and transmitted, particularly by those who are more dominant and powerful. Those within a devalued ethnic culture share the experiences of social inequality and deprivation and personal challenges that result from both overt and covert prejudice, stereotypes, and discrimination. D. W. Sue (2007) and his colleagues have called attention to the microaggressions experienced daily by people of color in the United States. These are brief but pervasive everyday snubs, looks, and gestures that communicate disrespect and denigration.

An interesting phenomenon is that ethnic stereotypes may change with the context of an ethnic group's location. Gilman (1996) suggests that Jews, for example, are thought to be smarter than people of other ethnicities if the larger society in which they live needs to see them that way. In pre-Holocaust Europe, Jews were seen as smart but unoriginal and parasitic. In contrast, a contemporary dominant stereotype is that Jews are intellectual but physically weak, unless they are Israeli. Similarly, Krech (1999) argues that our naïve image of the American Indian as an ecological preserver of the environment is unsubstantiated by close examination of the reality of American Indian life and their use of animals and plants.

There are now more and more frequent media accounts of mixed ethnicities and complex ancestries and identities (e.g., "The new face of race," 2000). Census data predictions are that by the year 2050, nearly 5 percent of the population in the United States will classify themselves as "multiracial" (cf. Roberts, 2008b). Among a sample of beautiful children whose faces appeared in the *New York Times Magazine* ("Race is over," 1996), we can see a child who is both Pakistani and African American, a child who is Filipino and Italian and Russian, and children with other complex ethnic identities. Issues of mixed ancestry have been brought into recent prominence by celebrities such as the golfer Tiger Woods, and President Barack Obama. Both present their mixed ethnic family backgrounds as positive features of their personal identities. According to the 2000 Census, 7.3 million respondents (3 percent of the population) self-identified with two or more ethnic categories, and 3.1 million couples (or about 6 percent of married couples) reported themselves to be inter-ethnic (Navarro, 2008). These statistics are probably underestimates since there are pressures on many to make a choice of one dominant ethnicity. Tiger Woods' description of himself as *Cablinasian* (Caucasian, Black, American Indian, and Asian) was not greeted positively by all (cf. Navarro, 2008). President Obama, the son of a White mother and African father, has chosen an African American identity, but has faced such questions as "Is he Black enough?"

Mixed ethnicity may well be as much a personal identity as Asian American or Italian American. Root (1996, 2001) suggests that such an identity is accompanied by its own special challenges and experiences. It is likely to be part of the multicultural uniqueness of more and more persons in the United States. And like other ethnic backgrounds its influence on behavior will vary with the situation, the interpersonal context, the time, the place, and the level of its immediate salience.

4

Gender

I hold women accountable for tossing out perfectly good men by not treating them with the love and kindness and respect and attention they need (Schlesinger, quoted in Stanley, 2008).

[M]en are socialized in a specific culture, with values, norms, customs, and expectations, to which men must adhere (Liu, 2005, p. 685 f.)

The focus in this chapter is on a category of relationship to other human beings that characterizes most of us throughout our lives – gender. Sexual identification at birth, "it's a boy" or "it's a girl," appears to be universal across the globe and is certainly so in the United States. That this recognition of a baby's sexual category is followed immediately and throughout life by the continuing development of gender, that is, socially constructed prescriptions and proscriptions with respect to behavior, expectations, and environments, is an exceedingly well-established empirical phenomenon (Lott, 1994; Lott & Maluso, 1993; Reid, Cooper & Banks, 2008).

The differential behaviors we learn as appropriate for girls/women and for boys/men in a given society and historical period constitute the roles identified with sex. Because these behaviors are, for the most part, unrelated to the few reliable biological imperatives or biological distinctions between the sexes, we use the word *gender* to refer to these human groups. The distinction between sex and gender has long been recognized within feminist theory (e.g., Unger, 1979). Whereas female and male refer to sexual distinctions across all animal species, the terms woman and man are specific to humans and denote gender – that is, learned attributions about characteristics, and learned prescriptions for the performance of appropriate behavior.

The first quote that begins this chapter illustrates the lasting strength, even in this 21st century, of powerful expectations for relationships between women and men and points with striking clarity to the existence of gender cultures. Regardless of her personal achievements or situation, a woman's obligation to "stand by her man" retains its prescriptive dominance. During the past few decades in the United States, we have witnessed a number of wives of prominent men in important political positions facing television cameras as they are humiliated by the public apologies and explanations of their husbands for serious misdeeds involving sexual behavior, lies, and illegal acts. We witnessed this with Hillary Rodham Clinton as she stood by her husband, President Clinton, during public reports of a relationship with a young White House intern and the subsequent political and social consequences. Similarly, Silda Wall Spitzer stood at the side of her husband Eliot Spitzer, the Governor of New York, as he publicly acknowledged improprieties. Ms. Spitzer, a Harvard Law School graduate, had put a promising law career on hold at the birth of the first of three daughters to assist her husband in his career and to care for their children. Governor Spitzer, a former Attorney General and anti-prostitution crusader, admitted to being a client of what was described as an international prostitution ring, and transporting a female sex-worker across state lines (in violation of federal law).

The words of conservative talk-show host Laura Schlesinger at the beginning of this chapter come from her discussion of this event. On her radio show, she responds to callers with advice on relationships. Her words are eerily similar to those in a "Marital Rating Scale" developed in the 1930s by psychologist George Crane. On this self-report scale, a wife could earn "merits" for 12 items that included: getting meals ready on time, asking her husband for his opinions, and having a good sense of humor. She would earn a "demerit" if she checked: slow in coming to bed, doesn't like children, or is a back-seat driver (cf. Joyce & Baker, 2008).

From the beginning of our lives, we learn what is expected of us as girls/women or boys/men, and to watch and emulate other persons who are most like us. We learn to repeat actions for which we are rewarded or praised and to avoid those for which we are criticized or punished. We also learn which environments are considered suitable for us and which are most available to us. Consider, for example, the typical preschool play areas of trucks and dress-up and where we are most likely see girls and boys. The conditions and consequences of gender are almost always inextricably bound up with one's ethnicity (and social class), so one's multicultural personhood begins at birth and continues throughout development, reflecting idiosyncratic life conditions and experiences and those related to group memberships.

All cultural designations are subject to change. One can move from one social class to another as a result of education, chance, opportunity, concerted economic effort, marriage, enlightened socio-governmental policies, and so on. Some people of color make the decision to "pass" as White and live in European American cultural communities, and some European Americans enmesh themselves in an ethnic community that they adopt, identifying with values and behaviors not shared by their parents. One can also make a public decision to change one's gender and gender identity. In this chapter, however, we will focus on gender cultures that are primarily heterosexual and mainstream, leaving a discussion of sexual identity minorities for later attention.

Differences in Relative Power

A feminist perspective analysis posits interpersonal processes as the major feature of gender (Gilbert, 1994). Thus, gender defines and is defined by the socially prescribed ways in which girls and boys and women and men relate to one another. Especially implicated in these processes is relative power or access to resources (Stewart & McDermott, 2004; Wingrove, 1999). The specific features of the interaction in most contexts will reflect the extent and significance of the power difference between the genders. This, in turn, is influenced by time and place and by the other cultural characteristics or categories of those engaged in interaction – especially ethnicity, social class, and sexual identity. Nevertheless, women's lesser social status relative to men's remains an ubiquitous feature of U.S. society (Lott, 1994) where, for the most part, institutions are so organized that "men are economically, politically, and often interpersonally dominant" (Addis & Cohane, 2005, p. 642).

Women's disadvantaged position in the U.S. economy relative to men's – in hiring, wages, and benefits – is well known and amply documented (e.g., Bullock, Lott & Wyche, 2010). A recent phenomenon is illustrative. Uchitelle (2008) notes that in the first decade of the 21st century the percentage of women employed outside the home is dropping, as women struggle with a harsh economy. He cites data from a Congressional study that suggest that women are dropping out of the work force not because they have chosen to stay at home with their children but because of layoffs, stagnant wages, and discouraging job prospects. The pattern seems similar among well-educated and less-educated women, married and never married, White and minorities of color.

While the past few decades have witnessed great changes within gender cultures, it is still the case that women and men are often excluded from what is considered to be the domain of the other. For women this translates into more limited access to resources, fewer positions of high status, and narrower opportunities for personal growth and development. Women's continued relative absence from high-level decision-making positions and lesser probability of economic affluence illustrate the sexism that remains an overt and covert feature of U.S. society. In 2005, women constituted just 15 percent of Congress and 22 percent of membership in state legislatures, with one lone woman in the Supreme Court (Hahn, 2006). In 2008, former first lady Senator Clinton, an affluent White woman who sought the nomination of the Democratic Party for president of the United States, was the target of demeaning misogynist humor and taunts. These can be sadly illustrated by the words of two cable TV commentators: Chris Matthews called Senator Clinton a she-devil, and Tucker Carlson said that he involuntarily crosses his legs when she comes on television (see Seelye & Bosman, 2008).

It is not accidental, but role and power related, that the incidence of HIV/AIDS has grown steadily among heterosexual women in the United States (CDC, 2007), and disproportionately so among women of color (Packard, 2006). In 2005, women constituted 26 percent of persons so diagnosed for the first time compared with 11 percent in 1990. Of the girls and women diagnosed in 2005, it was estimated that 71 percent had become infected as a result of high-risk heterosexual contact. The intersections between gender and ethnicity emerge clearly from comparing the percentages of newly diagnosed White women (17 percent) with newly diagnosed Black women (66 percent) (Diallo, 2008).

Cultures of Gender

The differential cultures of girls/women and boys/men can be distinguished by what they learn to do, believe, and value and by their significant common experiences in everyday life. These experiences take place in families as daughters or sons or mothers or fathers, in schools, in romantic relationships, in occupational and skill preparation, as consumers, and as community participants. Both women and men (girls and boys) learn continuously from birth the behaviors that are appropriate and inappropriate for their gender (Lott, 1994). As we grow older and experience changed circumstances in our lives, the earlier lessons may be negated and contradicted, or reinforced and affirmed. Variations in what we learn and what we do are tied to place, parental background, and special circumstances. Thus, we can integrate into our perception of Sarah Palin, the 2008 Republican vice-presidential candidate, that she likes expensive clothes and make-up, is a wife and mother, and also knows how to hunt, skin a moose, compete, and talk tough. A news story ("Alaska's uniqueness," 2008) suggests that Palin be viewed as a woman, a Governor, and also, importantly, as an Alaskan. How women and men behave depends on the historical, economic, and social conditions of their lives, but almost always as well in contexts where social practices are differentiated by gender, that is, under gendered conditions. Sarah Palin was carefully presented to the voting public as an outspoken Alaskan who was a former beauty queen and is now a devoted and compassionate mother of five.

The cultural aspects of gender are confirmed by studies of contemporary (as well as historical) institutions – the schools, mass media, religion, family, and politics (e.g., Denmark & Paludi, 2008). Despite great societal changes in the past several decades, expectations are still not the same for women and men, and significant consequences to the individual follow from both conformity and deviation. Gender still organizes social life and thus much of individual experience. Sarah Palin described herself as a former hockey-mom and member of the PTA, while describing her husband as a steel worker and snowmobile racer. Particular life conditions remain systematically related – by cultural prescription, regulation, or arrangement – to being born female or male. These conditions contribute to learning how to behave like a girl/woman or boy/man, although there are variations in these conditions during different periods of our lives and across groups differing in ethnicity, social class, and place.

In U.S. society, our gender culture can be identified and described by how we dress, what we are expected to like and dislike, what vocations are considered most suitable, what behaviors are typically expected of us, what knowledge we are assumed to possess, and what skills we are supposed to have mastered. Reid, Cooper, and Banks (2008, p. 260) remind us that, even today, girls across social categories "are expected to be interested in babies, to develop verbal skills, and be more nurturing, quieter, and more disciplined than boys." It is still not the norm for a man to sew missing buttons on his shirt or to be seen to cry in the presence of others; or for a woman to be turned to for advice on how to fix a malfunctioning car engine or to converse with another woman about big league sports. One still expects that most nurses will be women, and most firefighters will be men, and we are intrigued by the exceptions.

Systematic scholarly attention to gender began with feminist analyses of women's lives, but recognition soon followed that men's lives, too, needed to be examined. Men researching "masculinity" have been influenced by feminist theory and research and by the proposition that "humans are gendered beings" (Smiler, 2004, p. 15), whose gender deeply affects lives and experiences. Carbado (2005, p. 192) notes that a boy must learn to be a man since manhood is "a socially produced category.... a performance. A script. It is accomplished and re-enacted in everyday social relationships." And manhood is accompanied by privileges. Carbado's list of 40 such privileges includes: not having to choose between a family and a career; and not being expected to have a small appetite so that one can eat heartily.

While change continues to occur (at different rates in different communities), traditional views of what "real" men are like are still transmitted across generations. Real men are supposed to be reluctant to seek help, to avoid expressing emotion, to be willing to engage in risky behavior and aggressive sexual behaviors, to be dominant, independent, competitive, goal oriented, physically strong, heavily focused on occupational success, rational and heterosexual (Englar-Carlson, 2006; Lee & Owens, 2002; Philaretou & Allen, 2001). Some argue that such a definition of what is appropriately masculine is narrow and restricted, with negative consequences for mental health.

Another area in which change seems pitifully slow in the U.S. is the deeply held assumption that when children are born, it is the mother who assumes primary responsibility for their rearing and for their health and welfare, particularly when they are young. A continuing debate is whether motherhood responsibilities take precedence over a career (for educated middle-class women). The media have been particularly eager to write stories about women who opt out of the work-force for home and family (e.g., Coniff, 2006). Reminiscent of earlier discussions, career women, it is argued, are less likely to be happy wives and mothers – more likely, in other words, to be the source of a "rocky marriage" (Noer, 2006).

Typically absent from such discussions of parenting is the role of fathers, husbands, and male partners (Corcoran, 2006). Countering this omission, Belkin (2008) in a recent article in the *New York Times Magazine* described the many creative strategies used by women and men who are determined to share parenting, despite the institutional obstacles of employment and social custom. Particularly important in gender prescriptions and proscriptions related to family life is the inter-section with age. This can be illustrated by an interview study explor-ing the markers for contemporary young women of being "grown up" (Aronson, 2008). A sample of young women from diverse backgrounds said that what they saw as important features of adult womanhood were financial independence as well as parenthood, with many hoping for romantic relationships that were equitable so that family and work could be balanced.

Intersections with Ethnicity

Generally missing from discussions of conflicts between work and parenting is attention to social class and ethnicity. Pugh-Lilly (2007) suggests that an important set of beliefs held by young Black girls, derived from knowledge and experience of the lives of their mothers and other adult women, is that "motherhood and work are intricately intertwined" (p. 15). Regardless of marital status or socioeconomic status, Black women are expected to balance the responsibilities of parenthood and paid employment, with maternal employment seen as compatible with being a mother (Hill, Murry & Anderson, 2005). This expectation is contrasted with that of the heterosexual, well-educated, middle-class White women who have been writing about and debating questions that pit pursuit of a career against being a good mother. The so-called "mommy wars" are not reflective of the experience and values of most African American women for whom, Pugh-Lilly argues, there is no option to leave careers or good jobs.

Two decades ago, Hurtado (1989) argued that the construct of gender refers to a process of social interaction in ethnic contexts. She wrote: "for women of Color, race, class, and gender subordination are experienced simultaneously" (p. 839). While earlier feminist theory focused on women as women, this position has been largely replaced by an appreciation of the significance of group membership so that women (and men) can be more authentically perceived within ethnic, social class, and other cultural contexts (e.g., Denmark & Paludi, 2008; Landrine & Russo, 2010). For both women and men, daily life is experienced simultaneously in all cultures of which they are a part, with the importance of each varying with the particular situation and the cues and demands that make one more salient than another.

Hurtado noted that although both White women and women of Color are reared from birth to be mothers and partners, each is oppressed differently by men – the former through seduction and the latter through rejection – resulting in the acquisition of different ways of responding. How *woman* is socially constructed, therefore, will vary with ethnicity (and social class). This, Hurtado (1989) points out, is reflected in differences in sociopolitical concerns. White feminists, for example, focus on "the unhealthy consequences of standards for feminine beauty ... [and] on the unequal division of household labor," while feminists of Color "focus instead on public issues such as affirmative action, racism, school desegregation, prison reform, and voter registration" (p. 849 f.).

While patriarchy, the system of male dominance in major social institutions, is a feature of most societies that have been studied by social scientists (Lott, 1994), its manifestations will vary with ethnicity. Hurtado and Sinha (2008) interviewed a sample of Latino working class men about how they perceive manhood. The definitions they provided were instructive. They "emphasized emotional connections with others, being open to change and help from others, being collaborative, and being comfortable with one's multiple ... social identities ... They defined manhood in ways that let men be *more than men*" (p. 348).

It is likely that many Asian American men would also define manhood in ways that reflect their ethnicity. Espiritu (1997) argues that Asian American men have been "excluded from white-based notions of the masculine" (p. 13). They have been characterized as asexual, effeminate, as passive, ugly, and lacking muscles and physical strength. At the same time they have been stereotyped as the Yellow Peril, dangerous to White women. Asian American women, on the other hand, appear in popular images as hypersexual, exotic, sensuous and promiscuous but also as untrustworthy or treacherous – in the form of a cunning Dragon Lady or a servile Lotus Blossom. Still present in the popular media are images of Asian American women as "war brides, china dolls, and prostitutes ... unworthy, and subservient to men" (Chin, 2000a, p. 7).

Popular U.S. culture offers gender stereotypes for women and men from other ethnic groups, and such shared beliefs inevitably influence gender relationships both within and across groups. The Jezebel image of tough and promiscuous Black women conveniently masks the exploitation of Black women by White men, beginning with slavery. Interactions among Black women and men in the U.S., and their perceptions and expectations of one another, are legacies of the conditions of slavery and the centuries of inequality, prejudice, and discrimination that have followed it. Patterson (1995) argues that African Americans have inherited a "poisoned relationship. Slavery and the system of racial oppression brewed and injected that poison, and poverty and racism sustain it" (p. 95).

Jewish women have been stereotyped as opinionated, forceful, aggressive, pushy, domineering, intimidating, loud, and exotic. Early in the 20th century, a dominant stereotype was that of the Ghetto Girl – vulgar, loud, and overdressed (Prell, 1996). Later, the most frequently invoked images were those of the Jewish Mother and the Jewish American Princess (Lott & Saxon, 2002). To the former is attributed nurturance, self-sacrifice, nagging, and obsession with food, and being controlling, guilt-inducing, and overprotective of her children. The Jewish American Princess is described as manipulative, calculating, overbearing, materialistic, spoiled, self-centered, vain, ambitious, emasculating, shallow, complaining, and a trendy clotheshorse. Two classic jokes are illustrative. "How many Jewish mothers does it take to change a light bulb? None. That's okay. I'll just sit here in the dark" (Schneider, 1984, p. 269). Regarding the Jewish American Princess: "What does she make for dinner?... Reservations. What's on her bumper sticker? I BRAKE FOR BARGAINS" (Pogrebin, 1991, p. 259).

Latina stereotypes are conflicting. One set presents Latinas as self-sacrificing, dependent, sexually naïve, pampered, irresponsible, virginal, chaste, and martyred madonnas while another set presents Latinas as promiscuous and overly sexual temptresses. Lott and Saxon (2002) studied the relationship between such stereotypes and impressions of strangers. In one experiment, hypothetical women (Anglo, Jewish, and Latina) were presented to adult respondents as mothers interested in running for office in the Parent Teacher Organization (PTO) of their children's school. A significant finding was that Latinas were judged to be more unsuitable for the job of PTO president than either the Anglo or Jewish women. This result is reinforced by other findings. Nieves-Squires (Bento, 1997) found that Latinas in academia were judged to have unclear thought processes, to be hesitant about oral confrontation, and to be uncomfortable in non-Latin settings. And Rivera-Ramos (1992) found more discrimination against hypothetical Puerto Rican than against White or African American job applicants by a sample of New York City business managers.

What emerges from research with White participants are beliefs in a macho image of Latin American men, particularly Mexican American (Chicano) men. This image includes being hypersexual, aggressive, prone to anger, an alcohol abuser, dominating, lacking ambition, poorly groomed, and uneducated (Cervantes, 2006; Nieman, 2001). The women, Chicanas, are presented as "self-belittling, masochistic, self-sacrificing, submissive, docile, bad-tempered, long-haired, promiscuous ... unintelligent, and overweight" (Nieman, 2001, p. 60).

Dominant ethnic gender stereotypes are widely shared beliefs that provide meaning and serve to organize perceptions, inferences, and judgments about persons. Stereotypes denote sets of well-learned beliefs that have social (if not empirical) validation; they tend to be evoked or activated quickly and spontaneously. Devine (1989) has compared stereotype activation to bad habits. I have compared stereotypes to illusions (Lott, 1979) in that their evocation as beliefs is almost irresistible, even when one knows that they are not accurate. These beliefs contribute to the content of gender cultures in that women and men anticipate being perceived and judged in accordance with them.

Gender Distinctions

To maintain that gender provides differential cultural experiences for girls/women and boys/men is not the same as subscribing to myths about "sex differences." Such generalizations are common and predominant in popular discussions, images, and understanding of gender (Shields, 2008). But, as Addis and Cohane (2005) note, pursuing the study of gender by examining differences is like "assuming we can only understand one ... ethnic group by comparing it with another" (p. 635). Another problematic feature of the search for gender differences is that the typical attribution is to women's difference from men, with the latter representing the implicit norm or standard (Hegarty & Pratto, 2004; Tavris, 1991).

Empirical searches for gender differences do not always find them, although even the slightest hint is eagerly greeted and publicized by the media. Many studies that have examined well-accepted gender differences have found previous assumptions to be faulty. When Spelke (2005), for example, reviewed more than 40 years of research on sex differences in aptitude for mathematics and science, persons of both genders were found to share the same cognitive capacities and to be equally talented. Similarly, Hyde, Lindberg, Linn, Ellis, and Williams (2008) analyzed test scores from over 7 million students in ten U.S. states in grades 2 to 11, and failed to find evidence of a significant gender difference in math performance that favored boys.

Research data do not support the supposed truism that women surpass men in verbal ability, nor that they differ reliably in communication styles. A full review of the literature led Burleson and Kunkel (2006, p. 153) to the conclusion that "men and women speak the same language." Leaper and Ayres (2007) found little statistical support for overall differences between women and men in talkativeness, affilative speech, and assertive speech. Some differences were found under certain conditions, such as being in mixed-gender interaction situations where men were found to talk more than women. Cameron (2007) cites evidence that men talk more than women in status-relevant situations.

Meta-analyses by Hyde (2007) of psychological gender differences in a wide range of domains have found little support for previous expectations. The most common finding is that within-gender variability is much larger than the average difference between genders. This is remarkable in light of the still dominant average separation between the genders in experiences and in situations deemed appropriate for them, beginning at birth and continuing through all developmental periods. Hyde (2007) suggests that we need to understand gender less as a person variable and more as social-stimulus variable. Such a position is supported by findings from a study of test performance scores by 15-year-old girls and boys from 40 countries (Guiso, Monte, Sapienza & Zingales, 2008). In societies rated as more gender equal, girls and boys perform equally well in mathematics.

The search for sex differences continues and any that are found quickly become headlined news. A study that analyzed personality tests from 60 countries and found gender differences was eagerly reported in *The New York Times*. The journalist, however, concluded that while "the old Mars–Venus stereotypes keep reappearing ... What's not clear is the origin of these differences" (Tierney, 2008, pars. 1, 2). I have argued (Lott, 1997) that a sex-difference focus supports the status quo by keeping attention away from a serious examination of the conditions that societies link to gender and of the behaviors linked to those conditions. Avoiding examination of gender-separated situations and experiences helps to maintain gender stereotypes and unequal power.

That the context can result in the heightening of gender similarities and the reduction of differences is suggested by the findings of a study of over 11,000 people in eight different parts of the world. Struch, Schwartz, and van der Kloot (2002) found, from ratings of 56 value statements, that within each of the societies from which the respondents came there were no significant gender differences. Within each of the larger groups women and men responded similarly to questions about the guiding principles in their lives, such as equality, pleasure, creativity, friendship, health, and peace. The investigators note, however, that within a particular society, women and men may well differ in how they translate their values into action, depending upon the salience of their gender identity and situational factors.

It surprises some and shocks others that some older expected differences in the behavior of girls and boys (or women and men) are disappearing. Data from large-scale studies in the United States now find little difference between teenage girls and boys in smoking, drug use, and consumption of alcohol, and girls are beginning to get into as many car accidents as boys (see Aratani, 2008). Such data provide evidence of important generational changes in gender cultures. But it is very likely that the pressures on each gender to support such dangerous behavior may not be the same. Teenage girls are still getting messages from their specialized media about how to attract boys, about clothes and makeup and hair-styles. How these messages translate into the growing rate of risky behaviors that resemble those of boys is an important research question.

Gender Salience

To understand gender as a cultural variable, we need to appreciate that while the life experiences of girls/women and boys/men are far more convergent now than has been the case historically, there is as yet no simply "human" culture devoid of gender distinctions. There remain, in most societies, as in the United States, clear differences between the resources available to women and men, in their projected life course, and in their day-to-day experiences. The dominant feature of women's culture remains the presentation and transmission of values, beliefs, attitudes, and behaviors centering on the themes of caring for and tending to the needs of others - children and other family members, including spouses or partners, and the sick and elderly – regardless of what else a woman may do. The dominant feature of men's culture is that it presents and transmits values, beliefs, attitudes, and behaviors centering on the themes of providing material resources for others and projecting images of "masculinity." These dominant themes are supported in all institutions of society – the family, education, politics and government, the economy, and religion. Yet, there are places and times when some women are just as combative and aggressive as our model for men, and when some men are just as nurturing and harmony-seeking as our model for women.

Divergent cultural content based on gender remains dominant and amply reinforced in the media images found in magazines, television, films, popular music, and fashion. Men's bodies and women's bodies are presented with different connotations – with the female body far more frequently treated as a sexual object (Breines, Crocker & Garcia, 2008), and far more often subjected to scrutiny and critiques in terms of desired weight and ideal shape (Zucker & Ostrove, 2007). The pants in a woman's pant-suit are different from a man's, and the wearing of a skirt by a man will raise eyebrows and questions about his sexual orientation. Hair can be cut in barbershops or beauty salons, but it is almost always in the latter that hair is dyed or permed and finger nails and toe nails are painted. And while there may be conversations in each, the content is likely to differ. We know well where sports scores and game highlights will be major topics of discussion, even among men who don't really care.

The film *Sex and the City*, about affluent White single women whose lives center around clothes, more clothes, and relationships became a box-office hit soon after it opened in 2008. It was flocked to by women of diverse ethnicity and social class as avidly as when it appeared for many seasons on television. Interviews on the streets of diverse neighborhoods in New York City (Williams & Correal, 2008) revealed devoted women fans from different backgrounds and socioeconomic levels, none of whom could afford $15 for a cosmo cocktail, or Jimmy Choo shoes and genuine designer dresses. Pennebaker (2008) wrote about herself and a small group of middle-aged White friends who said they went to the film to see "[t]he stilettos, the gossamer dresses, the floral splashes, the tight jackets, the outré hats, the clutch purses, the hair, the makeup, the dazzling jewelry" (para. 5). In contrast was a news report at about the same time of a new combat sport, "ultimate fighting" (previously known as human cockfighting), that is apparently soaring in popularity among young men (Brick, 2008).

While the past few decades have been accompanied by a vast array of significant changes in gender experiences, opportunities, and expectations, gender remains a paramount component of one's personal identity and one's multicultural character. To understand behavior, we need to appreciate the significance of the antecedents, consequences, and complexities of gender socialization as it affects development and continues throughout adult life (Lott & Maluso, 1993; Reid, 2002). The salience and influence of gender on behavior will, of course, vary with person and situation, with time, place, experience, and context. It is likely, however, that gender in the United States rarely stands alone as an identity, and that other group memberships are always strong intersecting influences on behavior, depending upon the issue or event. This is an important empirical question.

During the presidential election campaign of 2008, for example, it was a sizable group of White (primarily middle-class) women who spoke with the loudest voices in favor of the candidacy of Senator

Hillary Clinton and expressed angry outrage when she lost the Democratic Party nomination to Senator Barack Obama. The media reported that these voices were sometimes joined by those of White working-class men who felt that their interests were best represented by Senator Clinton. At the same time, we are not surprised that, in 2008, a woman and her same-gender friends might be discussing a mutually enjoyed daytime serial watched during lunch or a new recipe, while her male partner and friends are watching a ballgame on television. While the same ballgame may be of interest to some of the women, and the recipe of considerable interest to some of the men, a gender separation is most likely. What variations there might be in terms of ethnicity, social class, or sexual culture identity are more questions that need to be pursued.

5

Social Class

[T]he social and material resources of a social class shape that group's everyday life and culture (Nenga, 2003, p. 171).

[C]lass is lived, reproduced, sustained, and challenged through social and historical relations, ideologies, and institutional structures of privilege, power, and inequality (Fine & Burns, 2003, p. 848).

In all but the simplest societies, there are divisions among families and communities by status, expectations, location, and power. In the United States, one is born into a family that can, with considerable reliability, be identified as working class, middle class, or wealthy both objectively and subjectively. This chapter is focused on the cultural dimensions of such broad societal divisions, particularly on the relationship between social class and power (i.e., access to resources).

One's membership in a given social class denotes degree of access to a society's resources – economic and political. It thus mediates and influences, directly and indirectly, what a person is likely to learn, experience, believe, and seek after. Social class represents sets of life experiences to which people must adapt and learn to navigate as competently as possible for maximum benefit and minimal injury. Ryan and Sackrey (1996) suggest that different ways of being human result from the existence and operation of social class structures and behavioral prescriptions.

The significance of social class is apparent in the empirically validated conclusion that it "continues to be the best predictor of adult educational and occupational achievement" (Jones, 2003). Class origin remains reliably predictive of what life holds in store. It is estimated that a child born to parents in the bottom quarter of the income distribution in the United States has an almost 50 percent chance of remaining there, and almost 67 percent, if Black (cf. Krugman, 2008). Recent research findings support the conclusion that there is less class mobility in the U.S. than we like to believe and, in fact, that our society is less mobile than it is in Canada, France, Germany, and most Scandinavian countries (Sawhill & Morton, 2007).

Despite this relative lack of mobility, "Class is not a central category of thought" (Bettie, 2003, p. 195) in popular, political, or educational discourse in the United States, and mainstream rhetoric continues to support a view of U.S. society as relatively classless. Nevertheless, other data suggest the seemingly contradictory phenomenon that we really do not believe this to be the case. Class awareness, though not much discussed, appears to exist (Stuber, 2006), with those who identify as working class being most sensitive to and conscious of class differences. In a study of college students, Stuber found that those from low-income families were more likely than others to report that "social class does matter" (p. 312).

Doing Social Class

As with gender, social class is a social construction, and can be described in terms of what persons *do*, that is, in terms of performance. Performance descriptors among a sample of high school girls studied in California (Bettie, 2003) were said to include such disparate markers as curriculum choices, extracurricular activities, "hair styles, clothes, shoes, and the colors of lipstick, lip liner, and nail polish" (p. 62). Social class, notes Langston (1988, p. 102):

> is how you think, feel, act, look, dress, talk, move, walk; class is the schools you attend ...; the very jobs you work at throughout your adult life.... [It] determines when we marry ... who our friends are, where we live and work even what kind of car we drive, if we own one, and what kind of health care we receive, if any.

Some would include what one eats and where one eats it: for example, "rich people don't eat casseroles" (cf. Tough, 2007, p. 52).

There is an air of entitlement that accompanies the behavior of the economically privileged that is apparent wherever they can be observed. I have often shared the experience described by Vanderbosch (1997) as she watched a group of preppy students in Harvard Square. There was "that air about them. That entitled air. That they had been born to inherit the earth ... the careless way they hold their forks, wear their clothes, snap for the waitress" (p. 89). Raffo (1997, p. 4) notes, "Rich people know what rich people act like, look like, and talk like;" and the non-rich know this as well.

Bettie's (2000, 2003) study of high school girls found that working-class girls, whether Chicana or European American, distinguished themselves from those they disliked and called "preps" – White, middle-class girls – by differences in dress and behavior. An in-depth interview study of a sample of Midwestern college students found that working-class students believed they could tell which students were more affluent by the way they acted – "their demeanor and the way they present themselves" (Stuber, 2006, p. 298). It was not just the clothes – expensive scarves, jewelry, and jackets – but the behavior and attitude. Consistent with such findings are data on expectations. Aries and Seider (2007), for example, found important differences in occupational aspirations between affluent and lower income students attending the same selective private college. The former looked forward to doctoral and professional degrees leading to careers as professors or in law or medicine, consistent with the work done by their parents. The students from low-income families anticipated jobs in teaching or counseling.

In one study, where social class was experimentally manipulated, the appearance and occupation of target stimuli were varied (Weeks & Lupfer, 2004). Middle-class male targets were given a clean appearance, were dressed in a sport coat with tie, and were identified as an accountant, real-estate agent, bank manager or high school principal. Working-class targets (referred to by the researchers as "lower class"!) were given older clothes and work shirts, were shown as unkempt and unshaven, and described as working as a delivery driver, short-order cook, garbage collector, or gas station attendant.

Unequal Access to Resources

Power is derived from access to resources. Therefore, the story of social class in the United States is a story of power inequities that affect every aspect of daily life. Social class position is associated with the distribution of political and economic influence and access to all essential resources – food, medical care, shelter, education, and income. It is not too surprising, then, to find that in a survey conducted by the Pew Research Center, 50 percent of respondents earning more than $50,000 a year said they were "very happy," while only 23 percent of those earning less than $20,000 a year said the same (cf. Ehrenreich, 2008a).

Each of us comes face to face with a remarkable (and well accepted) symbol of class divisions in the U.S. when we board airplanes that put first-class (or "business class") passengers *first* in boarding time and all amenities – including seat room, pillows, four-course meals served on china, and a choice of wine. Recent cost-cutting measures have affected the meals and wine. At some airports, first-class passengers are sent ahead of others in security lines. On recent United Airlines flights, I was amused and disheartened to notice that first-class passengers had red carpets to walk on when entering the departure gates – silly but discomfortingly symbolic. An American Airlines director is quoted for a newspaper article (Higgins, 2007) as saying "We certainly provide a great deal of attention to passengers willing to pay the premium price."

According to data from the Internal Revenue Service, in 2005, incomes above $100,000 were in the top 10 percent of annual earnings. The wealthiest 1 percent in this group, with incomes above $348,000, earned 21.2 percent of all income while the entire bottom half of the income distribution earned 12.8 percent (cf. Ip, 2007). The top tenth of the highest earning 1 percent (300,000 individuals) had nearly as much income as the 150 million Americans who comprise the economic lower half (Johnston, 2007b). In 2008, the highest rate at which U.S. incomes could be taxed was 35 percent, in sharp contrast to what it was for most of the middle of the last century, when incomes above $400,000 could be taxed at 90 percent. In 2005, taxpayers who made more than $1 million paid only 23 percent in federal taxes ("Plutocracy reborn," 2008). And, according to the Government Accountability Office, two-thirds of all U.S. corporations paid no federal income taxes from 1998 through 2005 (cf. Browning, 2008), taking advantage of legal tax-code allowances and deductions.

Financial earnings by corporate CEOs have frequently been almost 300 times the earnings of average workers (Krugman, 2006), so that "by 2005, the typical CEO made more in an hour than a minimum-wage worker made in a month" (Sawhill & Morton, 2007). Surpassing the top five corporate CEOs in 2006, whose total annual compensation was $290,456,558, was the average compensation of the top five hedge-fund managers – $12,600,000,000 ("Plutocracy reborn," 2008).

Some illustrative median hourly wages in 2008 help sharpen the meaning of economic inequality: retail salesperson – $10.33; customer service representative – $14.32; public school teacher – $23.29; and staff nurse/RN – $28.85 (Your Money, 2008). The annual median income for home health care workers is $19,000 and the Supreme Court ruled in 2007 that they were not entitled to either overtime pay or the minimum wage. Thus, it is perhaps not surprising to learn, from data gathered from a 30-country study by the Organization for Economic Cooperation and Development, that the United States had the highest rate of inequality and poverty after Mexico and Turkey (cf. Vandore & Keller, 2008), higher than such countries as South Korea, Japan, Canada, France, and Sweden.

Family earnings remain correlated with family ethnicity. Median household incomes in 2006 reported by the Census Bureau (cf. Edney, 2007) were $52,400 for White families, $37, 800 for Hispanic families, and $32,000 for Black families. In 2007, the overall median income was $50,233 (Sherman, Greenstein & Parrott, 2008). Home ownership among Blacks is 47 percent, among Latinos 49.7 percent, while it is 75 percent among Whites (Muhammad, 2008). The subprime mortgage crisis of 2008 has hit minorities of color the hardest.

Ideology and material conditions reinforce each other to both produce and maintain inequality (Bullock & Lott, 2009). In 2006, the Census Bureau's index of inequality (the Gini index) was the highest on record, with the top 5 percent of households receiving 22.3 percent of national income (Center on Budget and Policy Priorities, 2007). The Gini index, which summarizes income distribution across all incomes, ranges from 0 for perfect equality to 1 for perfect inequality. In 2006, it was .47 (DeNavas-Walt, Proctor, Smith & U.S. Census Bureau, 2007).

As much as 25 percent of school age children in the United States, and 18 percent of all children, live in families below the poverty line (Johnson & Johnson, 2006). In 2007, the poverty threshold was $21,200 (or $1,770 a month) for a family of four (Sherman, Greenstein & Parrott, 2008). Among the 300 million inhabitants of the U.S. are 37 million of all ages who live in poverty (about 12.5 percent) and 15.6 million who live in "deep poverty" – below half the poverty line (Sherman, Greenstein & Parrott, 2008). An additional 60 million live just above the poverty line in households subsisting on $20,000 to

$40,000 a year for a family of four (Herbert, 2008a). In these households, at least one adult is employed outside the home.

There is considerable criticism of the way that the federal poverty threshold is calculated since it seriously underestimates the number who are poor. Established in 1964 by the Social Security Administration, the level is obtained by multiplying by three the amount a family is said to need for basic, minimally adequate, food. Today, however, food costs are one-seventh of a family's income, while there are additional financial demands – for child care, health care, and transportation, for example, that are not taken into account, and higher costs for housing. The typical apartment rental price across all regions of the country was $737 per month in 2005 (Sherman, Greenstein & Parrott, 2008). Critics such as the Columbia University National Center for Children in Poverty maintain that families need twice the calculated official poverty level to meet their basic needs (cf. Satyanarayana, 2008).

Inequality in access to resources is seen clearly in statistical data. To appreciate the significance of such data for day-to-day living, however, it is necessary to actually "see" the workers who are part of what Bernhardt (2007) calls the "invisible economy." These are the grocery store clerks, dry-cleaner clerks, food service workers, hotel maids, dish washers, health care aides, laundry workers and countless others who are underpaid, are not covered by worker protection laws, are not members of unions, and are largely unseen by those they serve. Social class as culture can be seen in a report of a summer vacation by one of the high school senior girls studied by Bettie (2003). Once a year, Brenda and her mother went to Discovery Park. Despite its name, this was not an amusement park, but just a park with picnic tables by the river. To the researcher, this was a dramatic "comment on the disparity between [the] … life-world [of Brenda] and the one middle-class students took for granted" (p. 105).

Among the very poor in the United States are families eligible for some form of public assistance. Following much public criticism of the welfare system and its recipients, talk of generational dependency, and widely held beliefs that the poor were responsible for their poverty, the Clinton administration championed so-called "welfare reform" legislation in 1996 in the form of The Personal Responsibility and Work Opportunity Reconciliation Act (PRWORA). This legislation mandates work requirements for families in a Temporary Assistance to Needy Families (TANF) program with a five-year lifetime limit.

PRWORA succeeded in lowering the numbers on state welfare rolls but it has not reduced poverty.

Working-Class and Low-Income Families

It is ironic that until the recent widespread economic recession while they were almost entirely absent from the rhetoric of mainstream politicians and legislators, and from the entertainment media, considerable public attention was paid to working-class people and poor or low-income families in the context of public costs and budgets. In this context, they are the subject of media and public policy concern and scrutiny, and social science study. Included in this very broad category is a wide spectrum of adults – those who work for wages (not salaries) at union or non-union jobs, blue- or pink-collar jobs, those who work full time at low-income jobs, those working part time without benefits, and those who cycle in and out of such public assistance programs as food stamps or Medicaid and whose families would not survive without them. In 2007, the federally mandated minimum wage was raised for the first time since 1997 – from $5.15 an hour to $7.25, the level to be reached in 2009 (Labaton, 2007). When the poor are thought of, the faces that often come to mind for many in the United States are those of urban ethnic minorities. But 68 percent of families below the poverty line in the U.S. are White (Moss, 2003), and they live in towns and cities of various sizes.

Research substantiates the conclusion that low income is reliably associated with a vast array of negative psychological, physical, health, educational, and political correlates. In addition to low wages – inadequate purchasing power – there are related problems that are not likely to beset those with higher incomes – frequent layoffs, job instability, and lack of incentives and benefits, including sick pay. Nearly half of the full-time workers in private industry get no paid sick days; among the lowest quarter of wage-earners, 80 percent get no sick days (Herbert, 2007a). In about 135 other industrialized countries a minimum number of sick days is mandated but, in the United States, staying home for a day to care for one's own illness or that of a family member means losing a day's pay (Roan, 2008). In addition, involuntary part-time employment with no benefits described the work status of 3.7 million in the U.S. work force in 2008, as full-time jobs were drastically cut (Goodman, 2008).

Low-income parents are often caught in the conflict between needing to work two or three jobs, meeting inflexible work demands, and having to deal with immediate family issues, with too few resources for effective problem solving. In talking about their lives, low-income women describe coping with discrimination, instability, low and uncertain wages, and trying to "piece together resources from exchanges, private charities, and state benefits" (Mullings, 2004, p. 56). Low-income families face a problem that is hard to imagine if you are middle class – until you meet with economic adversity – and that is how to feed a family with sufficient, and good-quality food.

A new concept introduced by the U.S. Department of Agriculture, "food insecurity," is an interesting and cynical alternative to the concept of hunger. It refers to a family's lack of ability to afford sufficient high-quality food to meet nutritional needs. In the United States, 12.6 million households (11 percent of all households) were described as experiencing food insecurity in 2002, which meant that family members had diets that were low in milk, meat, grains, vegetables, fruit, and minerals (cf. Mozes, 2008). Substituted are less expensive empty-calorie foods high in sugar and starch. A correlation between obesity and social class is thus understandable. While families with incomes that are 130 percent of the poverty level are eligible for federal food stamps under a program begun in 1964, half of such families are not receiving them. The reasons for this include lack of information about benefits and unclear eligibility rules (Hotokainen, 2007). In my state (Rhode Island), food stamp recipients are subjected to a discouraging bureaucracy, needing to re-enroll every 6 months, having to fill out lengthy forms, and being offered difficult hours and sites for sign-up.

The conditions of working-class and low-income life shape daily experience in myriad ways, in intersection always with ethnicity, age, and particular contexts – the schools, the health care system, the law, and so on. The most significant aspect of this daily experience is exclusion from mainstream opportunities since working-class and poor people are outsiders who face barriers to crucial resources, discrimination, stigmatization, and stereotyped beliefs (Lott & Bullock, 2007).

Housing

Low-income families cannot readily afford to buy a home. Using my state of Rhode Island as an example, it was estimated that the lowest priced housing market in 2005 required an annual income of $63,441 ("Income needed," 2006). The mortgage crisis of the first decade of the 21st century hit poor communities the hardest and caused the largest loss of wealth for minority homeowners in U.S. history (Singletary, 2008). The effect of this on prospects for realizing the "American dream" of economic security, symbolized by home ownership, is devastating. Lenders in the mortgage industry took advantage of aspirations to offer complex, deviously presented, unclear, and dishonest mortgage contracts to poor and minority families.

Between 2000 and 2007, high-cost sub-prime loans were made to 55 percent of Black borrowers compared with 17 percent of White borrowers (cf. Singletary, 2008). The irony of these data, and their consequences, is captured by a cartoon (Wasserman, 2008) that first appeared in *The Boston Globe*. Two men in business suits are hurrying away from a disaster scene in which people and household objects have been buried. The scene is labeled "Housing Collapse," and the men are carrying a briefcase labeled "Predatory Lenders." One man says to the other "See what happens when you try to help poor people!" Ehrenrich (2008b) answers the question of why so many turned to sub-prime mortgages by pointing to the low wages received by 25 to 30 percent of the population, a figure more than twice the percentage counted as poor by the federal government.

A related pressing issue that affects low-income families is the scant availability of affordable rental housing. This is a nationwide urban and rural problem. The federal Department of Housing and Urban Development reported that, in 2005, 6 million households lived in substandard housing or had to use most of their monthly income to pay for housing (cf. Pugh, 2007). These families received no federal rent assistance. There are long waiting lists for housing subsidies (sometimes two or three years) that currently go to only 25 percent of eligible families. Low-income families are victims of "urban renewal" or gentrification, "the process of neighborhood change in which poor, urban neighborhoods are refurbished through influx of capital and middle class residents" (Goodsell, 2008, p. 539). Low-income residents are forced out of their communities to make way for trendy restaurants, boutiques, and tenants who can afford higher rents or the purchase of a home.

Education

If education is the route to a good life, poor children are handicapped from the very beginning, and continue to be shortchanged in school (Bullock & Lott, 2009; Fine & Burns, 2003; Fine & Weiss, 2003; Lott, 2001). U.S. public schools contribute less to the development of potential talent and skills among all students and more to "assigning desired future places in our society to the already privileged and getting the losers to blame themselves rather than the injustices of social class" (Raines & McAdams, 2006, p. 47). Contributing to this outcome are structural inequalities that impact schools as well as the failure of schools to confront the existence of social class. This subject is rarely addressed in school curricula or teacher education, and educators typically ignore the connection between schools and the rest of society (Kincheloe & Steinberg, 2007).

Yet, social class predicts teacher perceptions and expectations of students and their families. Low-income parents are widely viewed by educators as not caring about their children's education, as not competent to help, and as not encouraging achievement (Lott, 2001). An experiment (Auwarter & Aruguete, 2008), in which teachers from five rural schools in a Midwestern state were asked to make judgments about hypothetical students who varied only in gender and social class, found that low socioeconomic status (SES) students were said to have less promising futures than the higher SES students, with especially low evaluations given to low SES boys. These data confirm findings from other research.

What poor students and their parents are likely to learn about themselves is that they are not as capable as others or that they are potential troublemakers or criminals (Kincheloe, 2004). The very resources that would enrich the educational experiences of low-income children are typically in short supply because of the ways that public school districts are financed. Data abound to support the conclusion that schools in low-income communities are "under-funded, with inadequate textbooks, under-credentialed teachers, too many kids in a room, and facilities that are deficient" (Fine & Burns, 2003, p. 844), including buildings in disrepair and poorly equipped libraries. There are consequences that follow from such inequities. As noted by Johnston (2007a, p. 12):

> Children who go to schools with minimally competent teachers, outdated textbooks, and asphalt playgrounds are unlikely to have the same

economic success as children who attend schools with master teachers, the latest books supplemented by music, arts, and laboratories, and expanses of lawn for play.

From focus groups with students in low-income public schools in Oakland, CA, Fine and her colleagues (Fine, Burns, Payne & Torre, 2004) heard about lessons learned that reinforced feelings of power-lessness, alienation, shame, and betrayal. Students who were clear in their expressed desire for caring and competent teachers and instruction were, instead, going to schools with inadequate materials, rapid teacher turnover, and non-responsive administrators. Kincheloe and Steinberg (2007, p. 50) invited their readers to "[w]alk in any school in a poor neighborhood or in an impoverished rural community. One can quite quickly discern the impediments to learning ...-broken windows, no air-conditioning, old textbooks, stark classrooms, little technology."

What students in an urban school in a low-income community get that surpasses what students get in more affluent neighborhoods is greater surveillance. This begins as they start the school day and have to wait to be allowed inside and into police-patrolled hallways. The message is that students in some neighborhoods are not to be trusted (Pastor et al., 2007). A report by the New York Civil Liberties Union (cf. Herbert, 2007b) documents systematic mistreatment of students in low-income schools by resident police who belittle, curse at, search, humiliate, and improperly touch students. It is clear that children in schools with fewer resources have considerably different and less positive or enriching educational experiences than those in schools with greater resources and, beyond that, are more likely to learn hopelessness and distrust.

The lessons learned by low-income students in elementary school and high school are largely repeated in institutions of higher education. Students from low-income families are only one-third as likely to earn a bachelor's degree as students from more affluent families (Lehecka & Delbanco, 2008), a fact that is unrelated to differential ability. Summarizing the available data, Duffy (2007, para. 3) concludes as follows:

> a student from the highest income quartile and lowest aptitude quartile
> is as likely to be enrolled in college as a student from the lowest income

quartile and the highest aptitude quartile. By the time they are 24 years old, nine in ten high school graduates from families earning more than $80,000 attend college, compared with only six in ten students from families earning less than $33,000.

In addition to a shortage of funds (economic capital), low-income students do not have access to "connections" or networks, and lack knowledge of higher education options and other components of social capital. Bergerson (2007, p. 112) notes that "in a wealthy, college-educated family, potential students are exposed to extensive higher education options. They, their families and their peers speak the language of higher education, understand how admissions processes work, and are aware of scholarships and financial aid options." As a high school senior from a low-income family, despite top grades and a focus on math and science, I received no information about college possibilities outside of attendance at a free public college and no encouragement to explore other options or apply for scholarships. Additional aspects of social capital not readily available to low-income students are learning opportunities such as those derived from summer internships, research assistantships, and study abroad (Konigsberg, 2007). Low-income high school students need to use their summers to earn money in whatever jobs they can find – affording them learning opportunities of a different kind. Two of my memorable high school summer vacations were spent in New York City working as a receptionist/cashier in a cut-rate optometry office, and as a billing clerk in a doll factory – each providing important lessons about work and life, but neither earning me college internship credits.

A study of elite colleges (cf. Leonhardt, 2007), suggests that, when considering applications, "[t]he colleges apparently put even more stock in the polish that comes with affluence – the well-edited essay, the summer trip to Guatemala, the Arabic language lessons. In any case, the poor lose" (p. 79). Not surprisingly, three-quarters of the students in very selective colleges are from the top income quartile while only 9 percent come from the bottom two quartiles (Lehecka & Delbanco, 2008). Harvard and Yale, in announcing a new policy to make their colleges more affordable, will actually make more financial aid available to upper-middle-class applicants. Harvard plans to charge students in households with annual incomes between $120,000 and $180,000 10 percent of their family income (Konigsberg, 2007).

This will put less strain on college budgets than providing full scholarships for students whose families cannot afford to pay anything (Lehecka & Delbanco, 2008).

Two-year community colleges are attended by 6.2 million students, over 40 percent of the undergraduates in the United States (Glater, 2008) and, predictably, these students are predominantly from working-class families. Many of these students also have part-time or full-time jobs and many end up dropping out of school. It is part of the general disregard in which such students are held that "[s]ome of the nation's biggest banks have closed their doors to students at community colleges...and other less competitive institutions, even as they continue to extend federally backed loans to students at the nation's top universities" (Glater, 2008, para. 1). Lenders, in making borrowing difficult or impossible for some students, hurt those who need the most help to stay in school. About a third of community college students seek loans of about $3,200 a year. Without such financial assistance, low-income students must leave school or take on additional jobs.

A two-year study of New York City high schoolers making post-graduation plans (J. Bloom, 2007) found that many working-class students were anxious and confused about going to college – with lack of money their biggest obstacle. "For poor students, ... the cost of transportation to school, books, and food loom large in trying to imagine themselves on a college campus" (p. 351). The average yearly cost of attending a public four-year college is nearly 60 percent of the income of a low-income family. Thus, poor students must borrow more than more affluent students, resulting in a greater pay-back burden, and greater fear of taking out loans. Financial aid forms request information about family cars, mortgages, and investments that may be meaningless and unnerving to poor students. Bloom heard from her low-income respondents that they faced profound challenges and risks in making a transition to college, a chance they would be rejected and have to confront "subtle and not-so-subtle messages about who belongs in the world of higher education and who doesn't" (p. 356). The reality of such challenges and risks is revealed by studies of college students (e.g., Ostrove & Long, 2007) that find strong associations between social class background and anxieties about belonging. Markers that indicate who does and does not belong in the college are both implicit and overt.

Health

There are extreme social class inequities in insurance coverage, health care access, and health outcomes. A report by the Government Accounting Office (2007, p. 9) makes the point clearly: "Health outcomes are worse for individuals with low incomes than for their more affluent counterparts. Lower-income individuals experience higher rates of chronic illness, disease, and disabilities, and also die younger than those who have higher incomes." As one consequence, the United States ranks as the 29th worst in the world on infant mortality, one of the most important indicators of a nation's health (cf. Harris, 2008).

In 2007, 15.3 percent of persons in the United States, or 46 to 47 million, did not have health insurance (Sherman, Greenstein & Parrott, 2008; Urbina, 2008). This number includes full-time workers and more than 8 million children. Among the uninsured, about 33 percent are Latina/o and 20 percent are African American (Allen, 2007). In addition, and less often discussed, is that 25 million in the U.S. with insurance have found it woefully inadequate. A survey by the Commonwealth Fund found reports of high deductibles and out-of-pocket medical expenses, as reported in a *New York Times* editorial (Editorial, 2008, para. 4).

> Many of those surveyed had put off seeing a doctor when sick, failed to fill prescriptions or skipped tests, treatments and preventive care. About half had difficulty paying their bills; many took out loans, mortgages or credit card debt to pay them.

Higher rates of all major diseases and mortality are found among low-income households. An analysis of relevant data led Conger and Donnelan (2007) to the following conclusions: health disparities associated with socioeconomic status are pervasive, and affect physical, emotional, cognitive, and behavioral functioning; and parents differing in economic resources differ sharply in the investments they can make in their children's well-being. Socioeconomic status is reliably and consistently correlated with health outcomes and disease, and the material and psychosocial conditions that influence this relationship begin early in development (Kroenke, 2008). Among the suspected correlates of the poor health of low-income people is the greater probability of exposure to air pollutants. Sicotte and Swanson (2007) examined neighborhoods in the Philadelphia area and found a positive correlation between a measure of socioeconomic disadvantage and a measure of toxic pollutants in the neighborhood air. Exposure to disproportionately high levels of pollution is positively correlated with rates of childhood asthma (Little, 2007).

When health care is obtained, low-income people often find that it is accompanied by degrading and impersonal treatment Jain (2008) writes movingly of the different treatment received by hospital patients with little or no insurance, and reports a study of primary care physicians, 90 percent of whom reported adjusting their clinical management in accordance with the insurance status of their patients. In one study (Kaplan, Calman, Golub, Davis, Ruddock & Billings, 2006), focus-group participants from the South Bronx in New York City spoke about their experiences of humiliation in interactions with health care personnel. They talked about long waiting lines in clinics, being rushed through doctor examinations, and behavior directed toward them that revealed negative attitudes. Little seems to have changed from my own childhood experiences in medical clinics many decades ago.

Here again, we see a complex interplay between material resources and ideology, with stereotypes about class influencing health care providers' perceptions and treatment of patients (cf. Bullock & Lott, 2009). In daily life, this means dealing with medical personnel who see you as a drain on the system, as someone who will not follow physicians' treatment plans, as non-compliant and difficult. It means taking children to under-staffed clinics with long waiting lines and staff that often treat you with disrespect and impatience. The Obama administration has made health care reform and efforts to achieve some kind of universal coverage a high policy priorty. At this writing, how successful this effort will be is hard to predict.

Everyday Life as Culture

In low-income neighborhoods, whether urban or rural, children and adults are surrounded by messages about themselves and their families that reinforce their relative lack of worth in U.S. society and provide little hope for change or transformation. An interview study of the childhood memories of a small group of women (Nenga, 2003) found, for example, that those from working-class backgrounds, but not middle-class backgrounds, remembered the shame and anxiety they experienced in situations where their clothing appeared to violate norms. When exposed to unfamiliar food eaten by those from other backgrounds, working-class women reported being surprised (just as I was to discover vegetables like asparagus and artichokes), but middle-class women reported disgust when they ate some of the food associated with poor people.

Being urban poor often means living in crowded, noisy, dangerous places in deteriorating buildings and neighborhoods in poor physical and sanitary condition without easy access to playgrounds and libraries. It means breathing in air contaminated by toxic pollutants, being more likely to have an insecure and low-quality diet, buying clothes in second-hand stores, and always being on the lookout for better housing. From the time I was born until I graduated from high school, my family moved five or six times in search of cleaner, newly painted apartments and the free first month's rent offered during those years. Being poor means being part of the "secondary" labor market, in which one is expendable (and easily substitutable), an earner of low wages with few or no benefits, no job security, or no realistic hope of upward mobility.

An irony of being in this category is how expensive it is. A Brookings Institute (2006) study of 12 cities documented the existence of a "ghetto tax." Examples included: having to pay for cashing a check If you don't have a bank account; being charged more for a car loan and insurance; and paying more for food and other products in small neighborhood groceries. In commenting on the same study, Eckholm (2006a) concluded that "poor urban residents frequently pay hundreds if not thousands of dollars a year in extra costs for everyday necessities." Being poor and employed means having to struggle to pay for child care. Most states and the federal government have cut back on child care assistance and there are waiting lists for eligible parents. Contributing to the financial and psychological burdens of low-income parents is having to pay the full cost of care and yet not being able to afford the high quality of care that they want (Schulman & Blank, 2008).

For some among the urban poor, there is an almost constant fear of community violence (Lott, 2003). If the children murdered in these communities were coming from affluent backgrounds, Herbert

(2007c) argues, the events would make national headlines and the situation would be seen as a national crisis. Growing up in some urban poor areas is like living in a war zone where some are routinely injured and killed and many others confront daily trauma and loss.

Moss (2003), who studied families and high school students in a mid-size western city, found common stereotyped expectations of poor Whites ("White trash"): "oily hair, overweight women who smoke, babies running around in diapers, rusted cars parked on front lawns, clothes hanging on outside lines to dry, black velvet paintings, and drawling southern accents" (p. 14). These are the same beliefs found by Jones (2007) who followed the lives of a small sample of girls and their mothers, migrants from Appalachia, in a poor White community. Though now urban, they were still perceived as rural "white trash." The adult women were judged to be heterosexually promiscuous, swearing all the time, with missing teeth, poor hygiene, and not fit to be good mothers. Middle-class students in the city studied by Moss (2003) described the high school students from the poor side of town as lazy, stupid, tacky dressers, misfits, and criminal. What the low-income students learn, Moss concluded, from school, neighborhood, and the media, are "who they *are not* and probably never will be" (p. 41).

Among the rural poor, who are even more invisible to the affluent than the urban poor, are those who live in isolated rural or suburban areas (hooks, 2000). The rural poor include farming families, for whom life and survival revolve around essential work 24 hours a day – regardless of age or gender – in all seasons and all weather (Willow, 1997). The rural poor also include hired seasonal farm workers who pick fruits and vegetables. The average annual income for such workers is $7,500 to $10,000, and there is no employer health insurance, vacation pay, or sick leave (Working Families, 2006).

Deindustrialization has had dire effects in rural, as well as urban areas. One small town in Oregon that lost its logging and milling industries saw wages go from $20–30 an hour to the state minimum of $7.50, leaving families dependent on food pantries and hitchhiking (Eckholm, 2006b). In economically depressed areas of Maine, seasonal work without benefits is the norm. Here the jobs are retrieving lobster pots, digging clams, raking wild blueberries, harvesting potatoes, and working in sardine-processing plants. These workers face food problems and energy problems. One woman, who spends most of her income on electricity and rent, told a reporter (Eckholm, 2007) that she cooks a lot of pea soup and beans, and cannot afford to buy storm windows for her trailer. *The Beans of Egypt Maine* (Chute, 1985) is a rich fictional account of such poor White families.

When unemployment figures are calculated, they do not include teenagers who are not in school and have little chance of finding work. According to Herbert (2008b, para. 4), "[t]here are four million of these so-called disconnected [and uncounted] youths across the country. They hang out on street corners in cities large and small – and increasingly in suburban and rural areas." They survive through legal and illegal hustling, continue to search for work until they become discouraged; and are hardest hit when the national economy worsens.

The threat of job loss or layoffs is an almost constant stressor for both urban and rural poor families. There may be frequent moves with consequent disruptions in the schooling of children and in neighborhood/community connections. Other stressors relate to keeping children fed and healthy, to keeping them safe in poor-quality and dangerous neighborhoods, having utilities shut off as bills go unpaid, wearing ill-fitting clothing, and not being able to meet children's requests for "extras." Such conditions are documented across diverse sections of the United States (cf. Bullock, Lott & Wyche, 2010; Lott & Bullock, 2007). In addition, workplace indignities are more often suffered by workers in low-earning jobs. Waldman (2007) writes about the practice of having workers urinate into a cup or hand over a lock of hair for drug testing, a standard procedure by 62 percent of employers.

Cooney (2006) listened to groups of women in a work program for mothers receiving aid and found that their perception of their situation differed sharply from those who saw aid recipients as lacking in personal responsibility. The respondents talked about "a lack of specific skills, an unstable labor market, and parenting/work schedule tensions as key barriers to self-sufficiency" (p. 231). They spoke also of how their attempts to preserve a sense of dignity in the face of hostile and demeaning attitudes and treatment within the welfare system made them vulnerable to a denial of resources. Very similar findings were reported by Laakso and Drevdahl (2006). Their interviewees spoke of emotional abuse and rudeness experienced at the hands of welfare workers, and the threats of economic sanctions. In the words of one: "'They just put you back in the gutter. And treat you like trash'" (p. 92). Ritz (2008) heard similar reports from a sample of low-income people in Tennesee receiving food assistance. They described instances of everyday classist discrimination experienced in many different situations. Illustrative of the negative attitudes held toward women on welfare are data gathered from a Los Angeles sample (Downing, LaViest & Bullock, 2007). Low-income women of color, they found, were more likely than middle-class White women to be advised by health care workers to limit their child bearing.

Not often discussed is the special stress in working-class and poor families associated with sending children off to war. The vast majority of the volunteer army is comprised of young men and women from low-income backgrounds who join the armed forces for the incentives of signing bonuses and skills training (Gonzalez, 2005). Some have referred to this state of affairs as the "economic draft." Of the 1 million active reserve soldiers, almost 600,000 enlisted when they were teenagers (Allen, 2007). Low-income young people can easily be persuaded that military service is a good alternative to low-wage employment and offers a chance for college. The Department of Defense is engaged in such active marketing with multimedia videos, visits to schools, and gifts to teachers, spending more than $4 billion a year on its recruiting efforts. Young people, mainly from working-class communities and small towns or rural areas, "sign up to gain job skills, experience, and educational opportunities absent from their civilian lives" (Zweig, 2008). Sadly, the military does not keep all of its promises. Signing bonuses have been taken back from severely injured servicemen and women and others who have been unable to complete a full term of service. Until the passage of a new GI Bill in 2008, the college benefits to veterans were less than adequate.

There is considerable diversity among low-income and working-class households. Bettie (2003) distinguished between low-income families that were "hard livers" and those that were "settled livers" among the families of senior high school girls in a Central Valley California town. The latter "had managed to acquire a degree of stability," while the former kept experiencing "illness, disability, and death" with which their few resources did not permit them to cope competently and adequately (p. 134). Some scholars (e.g., Adair, 2005; Langston, 1988) argue that there are important distinctions between the working class and the poor. Adair notes that "many working-class families do have health care, own their modest homes, eat regular meals, take occasional vacations, [and] send some of their children to college" (p. 36).

Because of the differences in these material conditions, the experiences of poor and some-working class families will be different, particularly when households include skilled and unionized workers. But in times of crisis in the national economy, as is currently the case, these distinctions get smaller. The vast majority of the poor in the United States are working poor. About one-third of all jobs are low-wage jobs characterized by no benefits, inflexible hours, and family-unfriendly policies (Boushey, 2007). And more and more families face the danger of poverty as industries close, jobs are lost, and families must accommodate to sharp decreases in their resources.

Both urban and rural poor interact with mainstream others who often view them and their children as lazy, loud, not too smart, and drains on the tax system. Negative stereotypes continue to be found among medical, mental health, educational, and social science professionals (cf. Bullock, Lott & Wyche, 2009). Not included in these beliefs and perceptions is recognition of the extraordinary and creative efforts made in poor families to stretch resources. A study of a group of gifted women who grew up in families experiencing economic hardship (Koepping, 1996) reveals their expectation that hard work is part of life and includes their memories of parents' efforts to make the fullest use of all possible resources. Some recall how "stone soup" is made from scraps and leftovers, something my mother was especially good at. Hahn (2008) recalls the shorts her mother stitched from potato sacks for her brother and sisters to wear during the summer months in Nebraska.

From memoirs and novels, less frequently from the data of social science, we learn about such adaptations to "hard times," and about the skills that working-class and poor children must learn in order to make progress within difficult environments (Nelson, Englar-Carlson, Tierney & Hau, 2006). I learned never to discard scrap paper, clips, and rubber bands – and I save them still. There has been insufficient systematic study of the strategies and skills used by low-income children and adults to improve their economic circumstances, and of the conditions that enhance or retard such efforts.

The Middle Class

Just who is part of the middle class in the U.S. is subject to debate. There is rough agreement that it includes those with median-level incomes derived from employment in well-paid skilled trades, middle managerial, professional, or white-collar jobs (Champlin & Knoedler, 2008). Some economists define the middle class by household earnings between 75 percent and 125 percent of the median income, which was $50,233 in 2007 (Porter, 2008). It is the nature of middle-class life that is the focus here.

A dominant perception by those of lower income is that those in the middle class practice exclusion, in their communities and in their schools, by means of subtle or active efforts to keep class outsiders out of certain groups or activities. The power to exclude is one of the privileges of middle-class culture. Langston (1988) notes two other important privileges: leisure time, and being able to choose a career or job in line with one's interests and personal aptitudes. For someone in the working class, employment is less a matter of choice and more a matter of opportunity and survival, with work hours leaving little time for recreation and little else other than dealing with family concerns. Leisure time, a middle-class expectation, permits exercise at a gym, planning for and taking a vacation, and attention to meal planning and relationships.

Liu, Pickett, and Ivey (2007) have explored (White) middle-class privilege, the essence of which, they suggest, is the expectation that you will get what you need and want to have. "Privileged individuals expect to be treated fairly in banks, stores, and work situations ... [and to have] positive outcomes" (p. 199). They present a list of beliefs that illustrate middle-class privilege including that: county or city services will be available to help maintain their neighborhood; they can purchase not only what they need but also what they want; they can do all right with only one job; and they have the right to judge those who provide them with services.

Some of these privileges are experienced early by middle-class children. In comparing two child care centers in largely White rural towns, Nelson & Schutz (2007) found significant differences in the style of care offered by centers in working-class and middle-class communities. Both centers had good child-to-teacher ratios, space for play, ample equipment, and a range of materials and activities. Yet, the center for middle-class children made less use of television, had a greater focus on language skills, and provided and encouraged more freedom for the children to engage the attention of and interact with both their peers and adult teachers.

Despite the likelihood that "everyone believes the face of poverty is black" (hooks, 2000, p. 5) there is an African American middle class that is considerably removed in circumstances from those at the bottom of the income range. A Pew Research Center survey found evidence of a Black class divide, with Blacks, by a 2 to 1 ratio, believing that the values of poor and middle-class African Americans have grown further apart, while those of middle-class Blacks and middle-class Whites have gotten more and more similar (cf. Gates, 2007). Hooks (2000) maintains that it is not uncommon to find privileged Blacks who believe that they have nothing in common with the Black poor and whose "allegiance to their class interests usually supercedes racial solidarity" (p. 96).

To be middle class, a status to which most who are low-income aspire, is to have access to sufficient resources for a stable and satisfying life. Yet, some see this as a precarious position in the United States, fraught with anxiety about "falling off" (Ehrenreich, 1989). Economists speak of the serious problems faced by the middle class – "struggles with debt, access to health care, and an uncertain future" (Champlin & Knoedler, 2008, p. 146). Middle-class families are becoming increasingly vulnerable to emergencies, just as working-class families have always been. The "crunch" caused by heavy debt to pay for homes and college educations has left less to be put away for the proverbial rainy day. Weller (2008, p. 46) notes that, in 2004, less than one-third of families "had accumulated financial wealth equal to three months' income."

Loss of economic stability has become more and more a reality, especially for Black and Latino families (Demos, 2008). A recent report indicates that only 25 percent of African American and less than 20 percent of Latino middle-class families are financially secure. When the data were examined on indicators of security and vulnerability, "only 2 percent of African-American and 8 percent of middle-class Latino families [were found to] have enough net financial assets to meet three-quarters of their essential living expenses for nine months if their source of income disappeared" (para. 10). Regardless of ethnicity, in troubled economic times, the middle class can be described as "the middle-halfway between dreams of plenty and nightmares of want" (Vanderbosch, 1997, p. 92). Such an assessment is at variance with the widespread belief that the middle class is not only the norm, but a secure place to be.

The Rich

We know comparatively little about the rich – those living in a culture of vast entitlement with the easiest and most direct access to resources. Beyond statistics on earnings, accumulated wealth, and taxes paid (and unpaid), our knowledge is surprisingly sparse except for media reports about the lives of its most visible subculture – high-earning, high-spending, and high-living celebrities. Howard (2000, p. 379) notes that "there is virtually no research on class identities of those in privileged socioeconomic circumstances." And, as Lee and Marlay (2007) point out, residents of affluent neighborhoods have the means to guard their privacy and are eager to do so, resulting in a very limited social science literature.

It is surprising and perplexing to learn that "the rich devote a smaller percentage of their earnings to buying things than the rest of us" (Reich, 2008, para. 7). They also donate a relatively small percentage of their incomes to charities. A recent study found that the 98 percent of families earning less than $300,000 a year gave about 2.3 percent of their incomes to philanthropies, while families earning more than $300,000 gave about 4.4 percent, and families making $400,000 to $500,000 gave away only about 5.5 percent (cf. Denison, 2008). Charitable contributions, of course, are tax deductible. According to Robert Frank (2007), a *Wall Street Journal* reporter who spent a year interviewing a sample of persons worth $10 million or more, philanthropy within this group is fashionable and very competitive; "they want to give their money away now, while they can enjoy the praise and control the process" (p. 164). There is a wonderful fictional description in *The Appeal* by John Grisham (2008) of a bidding duel at an art museum auction between the CEO of a chemical company and a hedge-fund director. An abstract sculpture of questionable merit and aesthetic appeal goes to the top bidder for $18 million. The chemical company executive who made the successful bid scours the newspapers the following day for reports of his philanthropy.

What else do the super-rich spend their money on in addition to buying art at outrageous prices? The 2007 *Forbes Cost of Living Extremely Well Index* (cf. Sklar, 2007) listed 2 lbs of caviar costing $9,800, 25 cigars costing $730, and three months of home flower arrangements for $24,525. Robert Frank (2007) compared the homes of the rich people he interviewed to hotels. One such home included an indoor basketball court, glass-enclosed swimming pool, and an ice rink; another housed a bowling alley, a 2,000-gallon aquarium, and a 19-car garage. My own personal favorite is the home in Manhattan in which the wife of a real-estate developer had a walk-in closet so large that it required an elevated conveyor-belt for storing and retrieving clothes.

One suite in Manhattan's Four Seasons Hotel is described as having "travertine floors, grand piano, health spa and remote-controlled bidet," all for the price of $30,000 a night (Feuer, 2008, par. 2). There are lasers in the bathtub that turn the water different colors, and the floors are heated. A 38-year-old manager of a company doing hedge-fund trading, who is also the owner of several buildings in New York City, told a couple of *New York Times* reporters about a $50,000 four-day holiday he took with three friends at the same time that the 2008 economic recession was making headlines. He and "his friends got around by private jet, helicopter, Hummer limousine, Ferraris and Lamborghinis; stayed in V.I.P. rooms ... and played 'extreme adventure paintball' with former agents of the federal Drug Enforcement Administration" (Haughney & Konigsberg, 2008). In one lounge in Manhattan, the reporters were told, "bankers continue to order $3,000 bottles of Remy Martin Louis XIII Cognac." And a fitness company executive said he and his partner are planning a commitment ceremony on St. Barts followed by a dessert party for 2,000 to 3,000 guests that will cost $100,000. Even in hard economic times, the very rich are spending money on art collections, lavish parties, automobiles, and real estate. In Providence, RI, new luxury condos were being bought by persons described as "above such pedestrian problems as the troubled economy and the faltering real-estate market" (Dunn, 2008, para. 4), for prices ranging from $425,000 to over $2 million.

Much in demand by the very rich are yachts, and the bigger the yacht, the greater the bragging rights (Kranz, 2008). Yacht owners tend to be business entrepreneurs, industrialists or big names in technology. And they likely subscribe to the same periodicals to keep themselves up to date, attesting to their membership in a very particular culture. One such periodical, the luxury yacht magazine *Showboats International*, reported that, as of September 12, 2007, 916 yachts measuring 24.5 meters (80 feet) or more were on order or under construction. The biggest yachts, able to house gyms, small sailboats, and helicopter landing pads, are most popular. A yacht that is 100 m (328 ft) long could be bought for about $230 million, and there are 2,000 super yachts now sailing that are over 36.5 m (120 ft) long. A former CEO of Avis Rent A Car owns a yacht with a mast that is so tall that it can't sail under the Golden Gate Bridge. Also requested by today's yacht owners are mini-submarines and helicopters. "Of course, that means adding a pilot and mechanic to the yacht's crew, but for the people who buy yachts, that is hardly a concern" (Tagliabue, 2007, para. 8). Tagliabue reports that some yacht buyers take advantage of low interest rates and get a mortgage for their yacht, while others create a corporation to buy their yacht in order to save on taxes.

In 1985, there were 13 U.S. billionaires; in 2005 there were more than 1,000. These and others of great wealth clearly inhabit a very special world of their own with concierge doctors attending to their health care needs, travel to private destinations on private jets (some with alligator-skin toilet seats), and jeweled watches worth hundreds of thousands of dollars (Robert Frank, 2007). Their language includes words like "household manager" and "personal arborist." For college students from these families, talking about their vacations may include the word "winter," used as a verb, not a noun (Ritz, 2003), and may describe skiing in Switzerland (Rhem, 2007) or snorkeling in the Caribbean.

Children of the rich are not sent to day care centers. Instead they are cared for at home by parent-substitute nannies who most often are working-class immigrants (King, 1997). At an early age, the children learn status quo lessons about ethnicity and social class. School-age children will attend private schools, where lunch may well be a gourmet treat. The Calhoun School in New York City, for example, offered the following lunch menu choices during the week of January 3–14, 2005: "green beans with shallots; veggie goat cheese, sundried tomato, and arugula focaccia; hummus, cucumber, and tomato on wheat bread; fresh fruit; and couscous" (Johnson & Johnson, 2006, p. 196). In a story about wealth in New York City, Traub (2007, p. 22) imagines a party hosted for a private school class at which the "private chef makes exquisite timbales" and one kid talks about the "box seats [he has] for all the Yankees' playoff games."

Using data from the 2000 U.S. Census, Lee and Marlay (2007) did an analysis of more than 38,000 tracts or neighborhoods in the 100 most populous metropolitan areas of the United States and were able to compare the most expensive 2 percent with three other groupings. They concluded that: "The rich are indeed different" (p. 786). The most affluent neighborhoods were disproportionately White, with an over-representation of Asians. The adults were highly educated and professionally employed, but the women were under-represented in the labor force. The homes were spacious, and were worth almost four times the median asking price for houses in all the other neighborhoods examined in the study.

Merkin (2007, p. 110) described a visit with her daughter to some of the exclusive areas in Long Island's Southampton. She, too, concluded: "The rich *are* different." The most crucial thing their money buys "is privacy – refuge from the masses (and mass transportation)." What their money buys is life in a gated community where there is 24/7 security and direct connections to the police. Their money buys a sense of entitlement, the belief that "it is both a right and a necessity for us to have more, to have exactly what we want when we want it" (hooks, 2000, p. 48).

Not surprisingly, the rich in the U.S. are supported by a general ideology that equates success with hard work and merit. We are taught that intelligence and ambition will elevate our class position and that class privilege is deserved and based on individual merit (Langston, 1988). Variants of this myth persist, despite social science data documenting that economic success is more reliably related to the workings of networks and who-you-know (e.g., Jencks, 1972). In the interest of maintaining a capitalist economy, the rich are also supported by tax policies and legislation written in their favor – in other words, welfare for the rich such as friendly capital gains taxes, guaranteed loans, oil depletion allowances, business deductions, and even government bailouts for troubled corporations. This is nicely parodied in a cartoon by Horsey (2008) that shows oil company executives swimming in a pool of cash called "Record Profits Pool." A lifeguard throws them a Big Tax Cut life preserver, saying "These guys might drown! I'd better throw 'em somethin' to hang on to!"

Not all who experience extreme economic privilege are White. In addition to athletes and entertainers, some of whom earn astronomical salaries, there are Black professionals and executives who own Rolls-Royces and mansions, and who are members of exclusive yacht clubs (Williams, 1999; Graham, 1998). In the first decade of the 21st century, Black men headed such powerful corporations as Merrill Lynch,

American Express, and Time-Warner; Oprah Winfrey had a net worth of $940 million and Robert Johnson, founder of Black Entertainment TV, was worth $1.45 billion (Lui, 2006).

Jack and Jill is a network of elite African American children's groups that accept only invited members; the children attend only private schools and interact with each other in the same summer camps. There are 220 Jack and Jill chapters in the United States (Lee, 1999). Within this Black aristocracy, people are in contact with one another professionally and socially, and spend summers at the same places, like Oak Bluffs in Martha's Vineyard, MA. They provide a network for each other and for African Americans seeking support for careers in politics. Boule, a national group of about 4,000 African American men, is said to include just about every Black millionaire, member of Congress, mayor, or banker. Links is a comparable women's group. Affluent Black Americans "form an extensive and cohesive group with distinct traditions and a strong sense of identity" (Lee, 1999, p. 8), for whom ethnicity is related in complex ways to social class. The novel *New England White* (Carter, 2007) provides a fascinating fictional picture of African Americans of wealth and power in academia, business, and politics.

Moving On

Resources and ways of life are different for those situated in various places on the socioeconomic spectrum, and it is understandable that low-income people strive to improve their life circumstances. The desire for a "good" life in which personal and family needs can be met with security and without anxiety, and one can live in a safe and pleasant community with dignity and respect, is the essence of the "American dream." But making the transition from low-income or working class circumstances is against the odds, and not simple.

Narratives shared by working-class people who have moved from low to moderate or affluent incomes, typically through educational achievement, are instructive. Some stories reveal mixed feelings associated with changed expectations; others describe efforts to conceal past class status or to "pass" for someone higher in the class hierarchy. Brodkey (2000, p. 20), for example, describes how, in her high school college prep classes, she felt "radically displaced" and as having had conferred upon her "honorary middle-class privileges" as she began to experience some of what she had previously encountered only through her reading. In describing her undergraduate years in "fancy colleges where money and status defined one's place in the scheme of things," hooks (2000, p. 42) recalls finding herself "an object of curiosity, ridicule, or even contempt from my classmates because of my class background." She felt shame about food, not knowing what others were familiar with. Hahn (2008), too, talks about the anxiety as well as the shame that is implied and felt in passing as middle class.

Like people of color who have "passed" for White, numerous narratives from working-class people describe experiences of passing for someone from a more affluent background. This poignant description by Berube (1997, p. 63) is similar to that of others:

> When we have entered middle-class worlds ... many of us have had to pass as one of 'them'; we've been invited in as guests or we've even trespassed without invitation. ... Class passing ... makes us afraid that someone will find out the truth about us and kick us out. Being treated as a *guest* – as a scholarship student in college ... seems to demand our gratitude and indebtedness in return. Guest status can make us afraid of being disinvited, expelled, or humiliated if we say or do the wrong thing. Class trespassing ... can get us caught and punished, then sent back to where we came from.

Brownworth (1997) recalls stories told by her mother of being humiliated by her wealthy classmates as she did all she could to "pass", with the end result of pain and sadness from being caught or from self-deception. And Mann (1997, p. 226) describes his feelings at a gathering of same-generation upper-middle-class White gay men. "As I sat there mute and uncomfortable, I felt as if I were about to be discovered, my secret revealed."

In an interview study (Nelson, Englar-Carlson, Tierney & Hau, 2006) of a small sample of professors who had come from working-class backgrounds, some talked about growing apart from their families, others about their feelings of ambivalence about "passing," made easier by the fact that they were White. A common feeling was that they were contributing to the silence about social class, and its invisibility, by not openly discussing their backgrounds and succumbing to the pressures they felt as graduate students and new professionals to "pass."

Personal stories reveal the difficulties that are encountered by low-income persons as they try to make the transition into more secure economic circumstances. Bergerson (2007) shares the frustrating and challenging experiences of a rural Hispanic student who needed to continue off-campus employment and ended up leaving school. A successful attorney, who grew up in the rural poor hollows of Appalachia is quoted as saying (cf. Lewin, 2005): "To me, being from an upper class is all about confidence. It's knowing you have choices, knowing you set the standards, knowing you have connections."

Moving from one social class to another means leaving one culture for another, since social class position defines experiences and many ways in which one views the world. There will be dislocations in preferences and practices, and relationships, varying along the dimensions of intensity and scope. In interviews, Aries and Seider (2007) found that among low-income students attending a selective private college, three-quarters said they were exploring social class as an area of their identity; this was three times more than was the case among low-income students attending a state college. While the latter were in school with other working-class students, the former were interacting with students from more affluent and privileged backgrounds.

As low-income people improve their socio/economic/educational positions, they enter a different culture from the one in which they grew up. In this new culture, they have expanded access to the resources needed for a secure and healthy life. They have more power to influence the nature of their circumstances – where they live, what they own, what they eat and what they wear, what to spend their money on, what they can hope for, aspire to, and take for granted. For some, a new social class identity appears easy to assume, others experience ambivalence, and still others continue to maintain an earlier identification. For example, it is impossible for me to cross a union picket line regardless of the specifics of the issues and the context. And my interactions with police officers always contain an element of fear and reminders of the less than respectful behavior on their part that I observed growing up in poor working-class neighborhoods. I am drawn to politicians whose roots were in such communities in hopes that they, too, continue to remember their earlier class-related experiences.

The culture of social class is part of every person's multicultural self, as a set of present and/or past perceptions, reactions, life circumstances, expectations, privileges, stresses, and challenges. Moving between classes can therefore be accompanied by an enlarged understanding and empathy, and can contribute to enriched analyses of situations, events, and relationships.

6

Sexual Identity Cultures

A sexual culture is a conventionalized and shared system of sexual practices, supported by beliefs and roles (Herdt, 1997, p. 11).

As with other cultural identifications, one's sexual orientation identity is part of an individual's multicultural self, its importance varying with the person, the context, the time, and other potentially significant variables or conditions. The extent to which it contributes to beliefs, attitudes, and behavior – its relevance to what one does and says, its salience and importance – will vary with the situation and with personal experiences. Its degree of primary significance is subject to the influence of multiple variables and will not be the same for all persons. Nor will it be the same for the same person at all times and in all places. We know that heterosexuality is taken for granted as the norm and is thus less often the subject of discussion and analysis than the cultures of sexual minorities. But each contributes to a unique complex personal mosaic with consequences for situation-specific behavior.

Heterosexual Culture

The heterosexual culture is so dominant, pervasive, and overwhelmingly present in all aspects of life – media, fashion, gender expectations, family and work life – that it is seldom the subject of analysis. We are accustomed to seeing heterosexuality displayed (and assumed) in magazines, advertisements, religion, social and legal practices, and all institutions. Heterosexual relationships are "socially sanctioned and validated" (Haldeman & Buhrke, 2003, p. 153), positively reinforced and rewarded. Thus, to be involved in a heterosexual relationship provides benefits and access to resources and is objectively a source of personal power.

Heterosexuality is taken for granted and simply assumed unless directly questioned or challenged. Media messages are directed to heterosexual observers, whether in advertisements, films, or popular music. Personal information about spouses and children are requested by schools, hospitals, employers, and insurance companies. It is not just "the statistical norm," but also "the only form of sexuality [or intimate affectional relationship] regarded by society as natural and legitimate" (Herek, 2003, p. 277). It is not surprising, then, that in psychological research, unless the focus is specifically on sexual orientation, we assume heterosexuality in our research participants, ignoring the real possibility that they differ in sexual culture and thus in important life experiences (Herek, Kimmel, Amaro, & Melton, 1991).

It was the poet Adrienne Rich (1980) who brought sharply to feminist attention that compulsory heterosexuality is omnipresent in what we learn from our social institutions, and strongly influences our intimate relationship choices. She argued against the presumed naturalness of heterosexual relationships by highlighting the multiple ways in which western society privileges and rewards them. Current popular television shows provide support for this conclusion and illustrate it. A research group (Kim, Sorsoli, Collins, Zylbergold, Schooler & Tolman, 2007) studied shows frequently viewed in 2001–2 by 8th to 10th grade students. What they found was that the women/girls and men/boys portrayed on the video screen were rewarded for complying with a heterosexual script while they were punished for deviating from it by being teased and ridiculed.

Herdt (1997, p. 168) describes the widely shared myth of the happy heterosexual that is "inscribed in television, elementary school books, movies, magazines, folklore, and the common experience of everyday playgrounds and supermarkets." Regardless of the myth's degree of reality, we learn that the happy heterosexual is attracted only to persons of the other gender, has his/her romance and marriage officially sanctioned, has biological children, and lives to enjoy grandchildren in later years. We learn to accept as natural and legitimate the innumerable privileges that are associated with heterosexuality. Carbado (2005) provides a lengthy list for men that includes being welcomed as a Boy Scout leader and being entitled to have one's marriage legally recognized. Despite the recognized legality of same-sex marriage in a handful of U.S. states, none of the major political party candidates in the 2008 election openly supported legal recognition of civil marriage between persons of the same gender, nor publicly admitted that denial of this right represents an unfair distribution of privilege.

Sexual Minority Cultures

Lesbian and Gay

Those who adhere to a minority sexuality are, by definition, outsiders. In the United States, a variety of historical and political circumstances have brought these outsiders together in both actual and virtual communities. This is a relatively recent phenomenon. Considerable multi-disciplinary evidence indicates "that rather than being the aberrations that Western science has held them to be, same sex relationships and cross-gender behavior have been present in all societies from the earliest times ... [and] been positively acknowledged by many cultures" (Cole, 2000, p. 153). However, it has only been since the mid-19th century that the terms homosexual and heterosexual came into scientific and common usage, followed by increased interest in, and literature about, non-traditional sexual identities (Greene, 2003). The development of communities has come later.

Herdt (1997, p. 12f.) defines the term "homosexual" not in the narrow context of sexual behavior but broadly as "a significant cultural category of identity involving social, political, and economic practices and social institutions that are above and beyond individual actors." This "different sexuality," writes Vazquez (1997, p. 127) "informs our sense of self, our spirit and passion, our art, our view of the world, our creation of family and community, and above all, our perpetual status as outsiders." Haldeman and Buhrke (2003) stress the existence of diversity – in ethnicity, gender, age, social, class, and ability status.

That "there is indeed a lesbian and gay culture" (Pope, 1995) is a conclusion supported by personal narratives and the data of social science. This culture, or community, often functions as a surrogate family (Haldeman & Buhrke, 2003). Although there is wide diversity in gender, color, political beliefs, national origin, and family background, members of this culture share: experiences of oppression by the majority culture; special interests; language; concerns for safety; and sometimes the fear of being "outed." There is communication among those within the culture and to those newly entering it so that transmission of values and practices takes place. There is special language as well as information about contacts, support, and social networks. Harper (2007, p. 808) notes as follows:

> The existence of a distinct gay culture has been supported by psychologists, anthropologists, and sociologists and involves language, rituals, symbols, and other culturally normative images and practices ... geographic living areas, economic and social organizations ... books, television, movies, and music.

With the expanded world of the Internet, there is even more opportunity to learn about the sexual minority culture, to explore, and to share. Identifying as gay or lesbian may be occurring at earlier ages than previously, and Internet conversations and interactions are providing a significant space for the discussion of positive experiences, as well as to talk about threats and experiences of harassment. The Internet has made possible the existence of virtual communities for sexual minorities, providing a relatively "safe place to explore identities, [and] come out to one another. ... It provides a forum for testing and debating ideas" (Russell, 2002, p. 261).

Gay men and lesbians develop friendships, short or long-term intimate romantic relationships, form family units, and raise children. While some of these life experiences and challenges are unique, others are shared in common with persons in the heterosexual majority. The sexual minority culture, that constitutes between 5 and 10 percent of the U.S. population, is a diverse one in terms of age, gender, socioeconomic status, parenthood, geographic origins, politics, ethnicity and sexual behavior. Haldeman and Buhrke provide a rough estimate of over 15 million in the United States who identify as part of a sexual minority community. Garnets and Kimmel (1991) suggest that what is similar among members of this culture is that being gay or lesbian is an achieved status that is recognized at different times in life. Gay/lesbian individuals must learn to cope with omnipresent negative attitudes; and must face family disruption when their sexual orientation is revealed since it typically differs from that of parents and other family members. Gay men and lesbians typically manifest extraordinary resilience in the face of majority culture marginalization and misunderstanding.

Some who study lesbian/gay culture describe it as a predominantly urban phenomenon in both leadership and content. "The happening places, events, dialogues, the strong communities, the journals, magazines, bookstores, queer organizing, and queer activism are all city-based" (Clare, 1997, p. 21). Many have described the extraordinary influence of communities like The Castro, in San Francisco where sexual minority cultural aspects are clear and abundant. Berube (1997, p. 59) has written about his own experiences of feeling part of an extended family and interacting with others who shared a special language and perspective. There are many other gay/lesbian urban geographic communities, perhaps lesser known to the majority culture: e.g., Greenwich Village and Chelsea in New York City; the West End in St. Louis; Chicago's New Town; Los Angeles' West Hollywood; Coconut Grove in Miami; and Provincetown in Massachusetts. "Gay- and lesbian-owned businesses abound in these areas, catering to the special needs of the minority" (Pope, 1995, p. 302). These include bookstores, clothing stores, restaurants, bars, and periodicals. While ethnic diversity exists within urban minority sexuality communities, it has also been noted that they tend to be largely (but not entirely) male and White (Nero, 2005).

Lesbian/gay culture is not entirely absent from rural communities. Especially thriving are lesbian networks (like Rainbow's End or Fish Pond) that are kept going by bookstores and group meetings/events (Clare, 1997). And, according to the U.S. Census Bureau, there are gay- and lesbian-headed households in nearly every county in the country (Novotney, 2008). Gay/lesbian cultural associations and networks are national and international with resource information distributed in gay guides. Communication and association are also enhanced within the major religious groups, as well as in political, business, and professional organizations. Regardless of physical location, gays and lesbians have special ties to gay pride celebrations, as well as to commemorations of tragic events like the 1969 Stonewall riot in New York City or the assassinations of Harvey Milk in San Francisco and Matthew Shepherd in Wyoming.

Members of sexual minority cultures are simultaneously members of the majority heterosexual culture. Brown (1989) notes that many gays and lesbians have behaved heterosexually during their lifetimes and that "[o]ur families of origin are usually comprised of heterosexual persons who participate in the privileges and rituals of the dominant heterosexual majority" (p. 449). Of particular significance within the sexual minority culture is the culture of gender, which interacts with sexual orientation to influence all aspects of behavior. Research findings suggest that although sexual minority partners in general appear to value relationship and power equality, reciprocity and flexibility, gay men share many similarities in attitudes with heterosexual men, and lesbians are much like heterosexual women in relationship behavior (Garnets & Kimmel, 1991).

More complex is the intersection with ethnicity since lesbians and gay men come from diverse regions of the world, and may have grown up speaking different languages and practicing different customs and ways of living (Greene, 2007a; 2007b). Sexual minority persons of color, by virtue of membership in two stigmatized and marginalized groups, face special challenges, barriers, and oppression in a majority culture that is both heterosexist and racist. Lesbians of color are impacted by sexism as well as racism and homosexual prejudice.

Especially important is the significance attached to one's biological family. Greene (2007a, p. 400) notes, for example, that:

> African American lesbians are more likely to maintain strong involvements with their families; more likely to have children; and to depend to a greater extent on family members or other African American lesbians for support than their White counterparts ... they are [also] likely to have more continued contact with men and with heterosexual peers.

Gay men of color confront all the issues associated with heterosexism, as well as those related to racism. A study of a sample of middle-class gay Black men in Manhattan (Green, 2007) revealed that the majority felt torn between their Black community and gay community attachments. Their sexual identity resulted in alienation from ethnic kinship and church ties with less than successful and full integration into the mostly White urban gay community. Experiences of racism were reported in gay bars, gyms, and other gathering sites as well as discomfort with dominant Eurocentric norms.

Life conditions for low-income sexual minorities may differ sharply from those who are more affluent. The median incomes of same-sex couples are found to vary with both gender and ethnicity, with Black lesbian couples reporting lower annual median incomes than Black gay couples and much lower incomes than White same-sex couples of either gender (Bowleg, 2008). Purdie-Vaughns and Eibach (2008) suggest that the normative coming-out model that fits gay men and lesbians who have economic advantages "encounters serious problems when applied to the lives of economically marginal [B]lack gay men" (p. 385). Many in this group claim a "down low" identity as an affirmation of both masculinity and ethnic identity.

Stigma

Our literature is filled with personal and research reports of the stigma attached to minority sexualities and of the harassment and abuse that accompanies the stigma (Glassgold & Drescher, 2007; Haldeman & Buhrke, 2003; Herek, 2007). This contributes substantially to the all-too-common shared experiences of gay and lesbian children and adults who must confront stereotypes, prejudice and discrimination, and even violence. It is only since 1973 that the American Psychiatric Association (followed by the American Psychological Association) decided to cease viewing homosexuality as a type of pathology and cease regarding sexual minorities as diseased persons (Silverstein, 2007). In Western societies, during much of the 20th century, homosexuality was viewed as a sin or a disease and "a sign of decay and moral chaos ... At one time or other, every imaginable ill and moral corruption were blamed on same-gender desire" (Herdt, 1997, p. 27).

Within U.S. psychology today, "homosexuality is viewed as a natural variant in the expression of erotic attractions and relationships, [and] the adoption of a gay male or lesbian identity is considered to be a viable and healthy option" (Garnets & Kimmel, 1991, p. 144). What remains, however, in the arsenal of the psychiatric/psychological establishment is the diagnosis of gender identity disorder, for those expressing unhappiness with the sex or gender assignment given to them at birth. And, as noted by Kitzinger (1997), lesbians and gay men continue to be oppressed in many aspects of their lives and to be the targets of verbal abuse, threats, and attacks.

In schools, perceived sexual orientation is found to be second only to physical appearance as a reason for peer harassment, name-calling, and bullying (cf. Novotney, 2008). To counter this and to provide support for sexual minority young people, some high school and college "safe space" programs have brought gay and lesbian youth together (e.g., Harper, Jamil & Wilson, 2007). The earliest sexual minority youth groups were started in New York City but have now found their way into schools elsewhere (Russell, 2002). Typically reported is that while culture of origin and history may vary, similarities in experience bind the young people together. "When any other difference was explored with them - whether race, ethnicity or class – invariably they would turn the conversation back to the things they shared, not the ways in which they differed" (Barry, 2000, p. 96). Among what is shared, sadly, is common experiences of harassment, name-calling, and ignorance that are serious barriers to learning. Whitman, Horn, and Boyd (2007) report the results of two relevant studies. A national survey in 2003 found that 75 percent of sexual minority students reported not feeling safe in school; and a 2001 investigation of high schools in Massachusetts found that 16.4 percent of sexual minority students (compared with 7.6 percent of all others) reported skipping school because they didn't feel safe there.

The evidence of institutional heterosexism in religion, the law, the justice system, and medicine makes clear that members of sexual minorities do not have fair and equitable access to these resources (Herek, 2007). Lesbians and gay men are marginal and "other" in the majority heterosexual world. Exclusion, the primary marker of discrimination, is evidenced by families who refuse to accept the reality of a homosexual member. Exclusion is practiced as well by the U.S. military, which refuses to permit lesbians and gay men to serve openly in the armed forces. Instead, it follows an unconstitutional, demeaning, and dehumanizing policy of "don't ask – don't tell". This policy, notes Herdt (1997, p. 33) "is based on the stereotype that all gays and lesbians ... are hypersexual and unable to control their own desires when they are living in close proximity to peers and comrades in barracks."

I have elsewhere defined discrimination operationally as distancing behavior (Lott, 1987). Such behavior toward a study participant identified as a gay male was reported in an experimental investigation of the interpersonal reactions of heterosexual men toward a gay man (Talley & Bettencourt, 2007). Regardless of measured degree of personal anti-gay prejudice, heterosexual men distanced themselves more (psychologically) from a gay work partner than from a heterosexual one.

More positive and accepting attitudes and beliefs may be developing as heterosexuals have more and more personal contact with equal status gay men and lesbians, see and hear about respected same-sex celebrity couples, and watch some of the prime-time TV shows that have begun to portray such couples in normative and sensitive ways.

As is the case in other minority cultures, "passing" as a member of the majority culture brings rewards and reduces hardships and stigma. It is particularly easy to "pass" as a heterosexual, the assumed orientation, and thus remain "closeted." The negative consequences, however, of lowered self-esteem, devaluation, and fear of discovery have been well documented (cf. Pope, 1995). Since heterosexuality is assumed and expected, sexual minority members must somehow find ways to openly identify themselves when they choose to, in a "coming out" process. This continuous process typically begins with self-realization and then includes the sharing of this realization with others, requiring decisions to self-identify throughout one's life with new acquaintances and in every situation involving personal and work interactions. Coming out is thus "a lifelong process in which choices about disclosure must be faced continually" (Haldeman & Buhrke, 2003, p. 148). This entails a psychic/emotional burden that is absent from the lives of heterosexuals. It may also entail a loss of socioeconomic resources. Herdt (1997) suggests that one consequence is that very wealthy, upper-class people from moneyed families are less apt to come out, fearing a loss of power and status.

There is an extensive literature on coming-out issues, processes, strategies, and consequences (e.g., Glassgold & Drescher, 2007). Herdt (1997) views "coming out" as reflecting the decision to join and advance the sexual minority community. Riddle (2007) argues that coming out also serves to challenge directly societal assumptions, and demands recognition of minority sexualities by the majority sexual culture. The deep significance of coming-out experiences is reflected in the fact that "Whenever gay men and lesbians meet, sooner or later they get around to practicing this ritual of telling their coming out stories" (Garnets & Kimmel, 1991, p. 153).

Bisexual, Transgender, and Queer

Sexual minority cultures include other communities than those of gay men and lesbians. Boundaries between these communities vary in fluidity and sharpness; their definitions are not fixed, as they continue to be in process and to vary. Recognition of these other sexual minorities reflects an approach to sexuality that views it, not as binary, but as on a continuum, as situational, malleable, and socially constructed (e.g., Blaustein & Schwartz, 1990; Diamond, 2008; Diamond & Butterworth, 2008). This position, Blumstein and Schwartz (2000) remind us, can be traced to the pioneering work of Kinsey who: "As far back as 1948 ... admonished sex researchers to think of sexuality in general, and sex-object choice in particular, in terms of a continuum rather than as a rigid set of dichotomous categories" (p. 340).

Bisexuality is the most frequently discussed addition to sexual minority classifications. Although it was a long neglected subject in social science, there is now increasing acknowledgement of its authenticity and significance (Rust, 2000). Diamond (2008) defines it as a stable attraction to both genders in which specific attraction to a particular person will vary with context, the situation, and other factors. She argues that it has been underrepresented in the psychological literature and is more common than previously acknowledged. Tongue in cheek or not, Atkins (2002, p. 3) writes, "Every woman I know is bi! Well, not all of them. Just most of them." Sexual minority younger people, especially, have increasingly taken on bisexual or unlabeled identities.

There are sizable numbers of formal bisexual organizations within the U.S. and other countries, many listed in a *Bisexual Resource Guide*. There are activist organizations, support groups, and social groups (Atkins, 2002). "There are bi cable shows, bi web sites, bi newsletters and magazines" (Leland, Rhodes, Katel, Kalb, Peyser, Joseph & Brant, 2000, p. 561). These cultural resources act as buffers to the rejection often experienced from both heterosexual and gay communities. The former consider bisexuals too gay, while the latter often view them as not gay enough. Bisexual-identified individuals face the possibility of negative consequences when they anticipate coming out "twice, once as a lesbian or gay within the context of heterosexual society, and a second time as bisexual within the context of lesbian and gay society" (Rust, 2000, p. 433).

Herdt (1997) subsumes bisexuality, along with other sexual minority orientations, into the one large category of "queer." Those who call themselves "queer," he suggests, see themselves in the center of a movement to resist the marginalization and classification of lesbian and gay communities and in the forefront of those working to expose the imposed heterosexualism of western culture and its power to define normality. Riggs (2008) uses the term "queer" to refer to a critical analysis that rejects binary sexual categories.

Others define "queer" as an overarching concept to cover all sexual minority cultures, since all present a challenge to the presumed naturalness and dominance of heterosexuality. Also challenged is the understanding of *desire;* it is proposed that this be viewed independently of gender or sexual identity categories but as pertaining entirely to *individuals* (Alexander & Yescavage, 2003). Stressed is the importance of recognizing that sexual lives are not stable but fluid. There is always "the possibility of change, movement, redefinition ... from year to year, from partner to partner, from day to day, and even from act to act" (Cohen, 2005, p. 23).

Increasingly, within the social science literature, the discourse on sexual identities includes support for the position that these are not necessarily or even primarily stable. Sexual identities can be unstable, changeable, and in interaction with social and personal conditions or factors. This "queer theory" proposition, while opposed and challenged by some sexual minorities, is found frequently in recent theoretical discussions, in personal memoirs and fiction (Abes & Kasch, 2007; Suresha, 2005). The concept of queer, notes Marcus (2005, p. 196) "foregrounds the belief that sexual identity is flexible and unstable." This view is buttressed by empirical support. Diamond (2003), for example, interviewed, over a five-year period, a sample of young nonheterosexual women from a wide range of backgrounds and settings. She found evidence for change in self-identification, in sexual attraction, and in behavior. Evidence for sexual fluidity is also reported by Blumstein and Schwartz (2000). Diamond and Butterworth (2008) argue that models of sexual identity that are dichotomous and essentialist do not do justice to individuals whose experiences do not conform to these models. They propose that legitimacy and attention be given to "the phenomenon of multiple, simultaneous, and context-specific" (p. 366) identifications and behavior.

Some define transgender similarly to the definition given to "queer," to mean moving "across or beyond gender" (Golden, 2009, p. 22). Haldeman and Buhrke (2003) use transgender as an "umbrella term encompassing a wide range of behaviors, attitudes, and beliefs that break gender norms and stereotypes" (p. 146). A "trans culture" has been identified (Raj, 2007), and its influence is becoming more and more evident. Taylor (2007) notes that transgender issues are becoming increasingly more visible and are impacting public affairs, policies, and social institutions. There is a growing transgender community made up of a broad alliance among the diverse groups of nontraditional gendered persons (Cole, 2000).

Quart (2008) interviewed college students in the "trans community" for a story in the *New York Times Magazine* on sex/gender change. She was told that the primary issue is not that of feeling that one has been born in the wrong body. Instead (p. 34),

> many students who identify as trans are seeking not simply to change their sex but to create an identity outside or between established genders – they may refuse to use any gender pronouns whatsoever or take a gender-neutral name but never modify their bodies chemically or surgically.

They see themselves as "gender nonconforming or gender queer." In some colleges, these students gather together in groups to talk about experiences, reactions from family, expected career barriers, personal questions, or issues within the larger community. There is some evidence that younger transgender persons are rejecting older labels, identities, and fixed categories in favor of an acceptance of fluidity and context dependent on change in sexual attraction and self-definition.

Lev (2007, p. 147) reminds us that transgender or gender-variant people have "existed throughout human history...and across all nations and ethnic groups." What is new, in the past two or three decades, is the growth of culture or community identity focused on activism, and advocacy for social, pollitical, and legal recognition. Most significant in this new history is the Internet. This technology has enabled communication, the making of connections, and the establishment of virtual communities by facilitating the sharing of concerns, beliefs, and experiences. Lev (2007, p. 163) notes that "Typing the word *transgender* into any search engine will reveal hundreds of personal Websites, blogs, line journals, newsgroups, and academic resources ... [d]iscussion lists and online chats."

Within the contemporary "trans culture" is a wide array of diverse sexual identities including cross dressers or transvestites, and women and men transsexuals who have undergone physical sex changes of some sort, involving partial or complete medical (hormonal/surgical) assistance. The term "transsexual" typically refers to individuals who feel that their experienced gender is not consonant with their biological sex and who "seek surgical or hormonal modifications in order to bring these two into alignment" (Diamond & Butterworth, 2008, p. 366). To qualify for such official medical intervention, an individual must usually receive a psychiatric diagnosis of "gender identity disorder." A task force established by the American Psychological Association on Gender Identity and Gender Variance recommended that the association take no position on this diagnosis because of disagreement about its meaning and the extent to which it is ultimately helpful or harmful to the person so diagnosed ("APA Resolves," 2008).

Whether sexual identity is viewed as situated on a continuum or subsumable under a finite number of stable categories, it must be "understood in interaction with other aspects of identity" (Greene, 2003, p. 383). Its salience will vary in relation to that of other cultural identities and with context, time and place, age, and socio-political events. Sexual identity provides still another cultural thread or ribbon within the flexible mosaic of a person's multicultural self.

7

The Cultural Mosaic

*The self [may be] ... conceptualized as a multidimensional struc-
ture that mirrors the multiple positions of one's unique interaction
network* (Piliavin, Grube, & Callero, 2002, p. 472).

*Every person is a member of multiple social groups, and thus every-
one has multiple social identities* (Murphy, Steele & Gross, 2007,
p. 879).

*[I]dentities change in meaning and significance in response
to changing social circumstances* (Clayton & Opotow, 2003,
p. 308).

Each of us, as a unique multicultural individual, has multiple social
identities as a consequence of our multiple cultural memberships.
These groups of which we are a part vary in size and location, and their
salience and influence vary with time and place. If we use as criteria for
culture groups of people who share history, current problems, common
experiences, language, values, similar adaptations or behaviors, beliefs,
and attitudes as well as the passing on of these similarities to future
generations, then we must recognize that culture is not limited by
physical proximity or by size. We can identify cultures as large as
"Western civilization" and those as small as a neighborhood gang or a
college. As a faculty member in a public university with a sizable com-
muter student body, I frequently asked my students to think about
how the culture of their school compared with that of a private

ivy-league university in the same state just 40 miles away. No one ever had any difficulty making cultural distinctions between the two.

In one study (Haslam, Rothschild & Ernst, 2000), a sample of U.S. undergraduate students were able to identify special characteristics of 20 social categories that included (beyond those of ethnicity, gender, sexual orientation, and social class): age, dietary groups (e.g. vegetarians), disability groups, political groups, and regional/geographical groups. In scholarly journals as well as in fictional and non-fictional literature, and the media, one finds accounts of youth culture, sport fan culture, occupational cultures, and so on. Brewer and Pierce (2005) reported on a mail survey of households in Ohio in which respondents listed their important group memberships. Sports fans viewed other fans as people similar to themselves.

These smaller cultures may or may not matter as much as those discussed earlier in this book. According to Frable (1997, p. 140), "the cultural categories that matter ... [are] the ones that we all pay attention to in our daily lives." What these are is an important empirical question. The cultures that *matter* are likely not to be the same for all of us and to vary across persons. The value or consequences of membership in different cultural communities will differ among us, even for those cultures that are most often studied and recognized as important in daily life. West and Fenstermaker (1996) discuss "situated conduct" and suggest that we ask which behaviors or reactions in situation X by person A is a reflection of which of A's cultural identities.

Not all "older" people identify themselves as part of a senior culture, but many are similarly offended by a physician who talks past them to the daughter or son accompanying them about their health, or by a store clerk who assumes that they don't know how to work a computer, or by being ignored in a restaurant, or by "elderspeak" – being called "sweetie" or "dear" or by their first names (Leland, 2008). Older persons share such incidents with one another. When shared with younger friends or colleagues they are likely to be presented in the context of "preparation" for those who will be moving into a new culture of age.

Diverse Cultural Communities

It is not possible within the pages of this book to do more than select a few of these less studied cultures for some brief discussion. For someone who is a member of an "other culture," however, membership in it may be of fundamental and primary significance with the extent of its importance varying with time, context, and immediate situation, from looming large and dominant to inconsequential.

Cultures of Place

There are cultures of "place" that have shifting consequences for individual behavior. Beginning with Newcomb's early classic study of political norm development among students at Bennington College (Newcomb, Koenig, Flacks & Warwick, 1967), research has documented the growing similarity of attitudes and beliefs among people living in close proximity to one another. In a recent study (Cullum & Harton, 2007), increasing similarity over time in attitudes on a wide range of issues, and particularly on issues judged to be important, was found among housemates in residence halls in a Midwestern university.

Residents of New York City can talk knowledgeably about the cultures of Brooklyn's Bedford-Stuyvesant or Williamsburg, Flushing in Queens, the Upper West Side, the Upper East Side, Harlem, and the South Bronx (to name just a few). These are neighborhood cultures that are heavily intertwined with social class and ethnicity. With the advent of Governor Sarah Palin into the national political scene, we have all learned a good deal about her state of Alaska, and its unique culture. It has been described as "its own world," colonial and frontier, big, wild, and cold with a special history, economy, inhabitants, and set of values ("Alaska's uniqueness," 2008). Cultural status is also attributed to other geographical locations in the United States, e.g., the Midwest, far west, New England. Those of us who are Rhode Islanders by birth or adoption can speak at some length about our unique words, pronunciations, foods, and foibles, celebrated and shared in stories and cartoons (e.g., Bousquet, 1997).

The culture of the American South has been richly and often portrayed in plays and novels. A recent example of a segment of this culture can be drawn from newspaper reports of how symbols of the old pre-Civil War South remain extraordinarily important to some. In the mid-1990s, in several Southern states, there were efforts to remove Confederate flags from courthouses, to remove Confederate statues, to change lyrics of official state songs or to replace them with others, and to discontinue waving Confederate flags at sports events or putting them on state license plates (Sack, 1997). Such efforts were met with strong opposition by supporters of the Southern heritage with which they identify. Groups like the Southern Heritage Association and Sons of Confederate Veterans defended the continued public presence of the symbols of their culture.

Disability Cultures

There were strong public protests within the past two decades by students and staff at Gallaudet University, a liberal arts university for the deaf, over the selection of a new president (Leigh & Brice, 2003; Schemo, 2006). In 1988, when the Board of Trustees selected a hearing candidate, passing over candidates who were deaf, the protest was led by a group calling itself the Deaf President Now movement. A more recent protest raised significant questions about deaf culture, including whether deafness should be viewed as a disability or an identity. Should American Sign Language be the exclusive means to communicate among the deaf, with professors required to be fluent signers? The use of technology to enhance hearing, such as cochlear implants, and the use of spoken language, present challenges to deaf culture and are subjects of heated debate.

Beckenroth-Ohsako (1999) argues for the legitimacy of a deaf minority culture in which individuals share a language, an identity, common problems and frustrations. In addition, deaf people share personal history, customs, stories, and jokes, and some define themselves as a "minority group within a multicultural society" (p. 114). Moradi and Rottenstein (2007) also regard deaf persons as members of a unique culture with shared experience, history, and language. Among those who are most vocal in the deaf community are voices calling for a perception of themselves not as part of a larger disability culture, but rather as a distinctive linguistic minority culture.

That there is a disability culture is a view increasingly voiced and strongly promoted by activists who have successfully raised consciousness about disability issues and access to public places, employment, and housing. There are close to 50 million people with disabilities in the United States, that is, people with some impairment that limits at least one major life activity (cf. Quinlan, Bowleg & Ritz, 2008). Those who view disabilities as a form of diversity highlight the existence of common experiences among the disabled (e.g., Leigh & Brice, 2003). As is true for many other minority cultures in the United States, members experience stigma, marginality, and discrimination, and are devalued as vulnerable. Scheer (1994, p. 251) proposes that a "sociopolitical definition of disability connects people with the broadest range of disabilities to each other by locating disability in the interaction of the person within her or his environment, rather than solely within the individual."

Political Cultures

Members of a political culture may be diverse in many respects but are held together by a special set of values, beliefs, attitudes, language, and behaviors. For example, Napier and Jost (2008) found important differences between conservatives and liberals in a large nationally representative sample in their beliefs about (or rationalizations of) inequality. Political cultures, broadly understood, might be said to include, in addition to liberalism and conservatism, pacifism, socialism, and feminism (Huddy, 2001). Numerous studies have found that feminists, for example, are bound together by common attitudes, beliefs, and self-identification (e.g., Eisele & Stake, 2008). As with other cultural identities, those based on politically similar views will vary in importance depending on the situation, context, time, and place.

Wellman (1999, p. 79) writes of his parents, that they did not see "themselves as ethnic nor ... as religious. ... Their identity was political. They were Communists. ... The powerful categories in our lives were not ethnicity, religion, or race. The category that defined us was politics." Some children brought up by left-wing parents have referred to themselves as "red-diaper babies." Persons who consider themselves politically progressive or left-of-center are spread across geographical areas in the U.S. but share a culture that is maintained and transmitted by membership in formal groups, Internet connections, periodicals, and newsletters. Members of this culture may get their news, commentaries, and analyses from *In These Times, Mother Jones,* or *The Nation* while those imbedded in a right-wing culture keep their TVs tuned to *Fox News* and follow the political guidance of commentators like Rush

Limbaugh. A small conservative political community connected primarily by the Internet was the subject of a *New York Times* article (Eligon, 2008). Described is a group of young Black Republicans calling themselves *HipHop Republicans* who maintain a blog of the same name. Another source of connection and information in the African American "conservative blogosphere" is *Booker Rising*. Political cultures, like others, can be described by distinctive beliefs, symbols, sometimes music, actions and attitudes, and efforts to transmit these to new generations.

The Culture of Singleness

The particular concerns and challenges faced by people who remain unmarried by choice (in a society in which this is considered to be a minority lifestyle) have prompted some to view single status in cultural terms. DePaulo (2006) has studied both bachelorhood for men and singleness for women. She found that "People who do not have a serious coupled relationship . . . are stereotyped, discriminated against, and treated dismissively" (p. 2). A typical response to a single person, she notes, is to assume that she or he is lonely, envious of couples, afraid of commitment, or too picky, perhaps even selfish and immature, or homosexual, and missing out on the emotional and physical intimacy that comes with being part of a couple. Studies confirm that a single woman, especially, is often marginalized, stigmatized, and seen as being outside of normal family life (Reynolds & Wetherell, 2003; Reynolds, Wetherell & Taylor, 2007), with the dominant message in Western society being that "emotional satisfaction, sexual fulfillment, companionship, security, and spiritual meaning" can only be found as part of an intimate couple (Trimberger, 2005, p. x).

Despite the dominant prejudice, Trimberger found, from her 2005 study of the narratives of a sample of single women, that they reported leading satisfying lives. Not being coupled has become a more and more viable life option, as indicated by U.S. Census data. In 2003, there were about 52 million adults in the United States who had been single all their lives. Counting other singles through divorce or widowhood, and not counting cohabiting couples, DePaulo (2006) estimated 76 million single people. Yet, the advantages and normativeness of being part of a couple continue to be assumed in the market place, in the law, in the media, in our institutions, and our social relationships. Persons who are single are often excluded by their coupled friends from outings, vacations, parties; there may be an assumption that a person who is still single is jealous of a married or coupled one, that "couples are special and singles are second-class" (DePaulo, 2006, p. 69). It is assumed that single persons are dedicated to exploring ways to find a partner and that, if they fail, they will grow old and die alone. Internet sites for meeting other singles abound.

But do the assumptions about singleness and common experiences provide a cultural connection with other singles? Some research suggests that ever-singles (women especially) tend to have stable, long-lasting friendships, to interact with others who share their interests, and to view friendships as important sources of intimacy and support. Ever-singles have also learned skills associated with performing everyday tasks by themselves. DePaulo (2006, p. 259) writes:

> My guess is that single people, compared with coupled people, are more likely to be linked to the members of their social networks by bonds of affection. ... The networks of single people ... are more likely to be intentional communities rather than collections of matched sets of couples.

This conclusion is supported by Trimberger (2005) who sees the family networks among single women, that include childhood, work, political, and recreational friends, as connections akin to communities.

Cultural Identities: How Do I Describe Myself?

Shelton and Sellers (2000, p. 27) note that "If you were asked to describe who you are ... you might respond in different ways, depending on the situation." At any given moment one's membership in multiple cultures will be relevant to the performance of any social behavior. But while "people are all simultaneously gendered, raced, classed, and sexually 'oriented'" (Rappaport & Stewart, 1997, p. 316), the relevance of each of these identities to behavior will depend upon the issue addressed by the behavior, its immediate context, those with whom interaction is anticipated, and the circumstances of the interaction (Phan, 2005). As I write this, I think of how I see myself when I am at my gym in an aerobics or stretch class; what is most salient to me there are my cultures of gender, age, and social class. But during a Passover holiday, spent at the home of my son and his family, what was most salient and prominent for me was my ethnicity. This became less significant during discussions of current social issues when it was my political identity that was most salient and relevant and strong. The cultures of which we are a part are not likely to have independent consequences but to interact or intersect as they influence what we say and do.

Cultural identity is based on group memberships that are accepted or claimed (Deaux, 2006). Some, like ethnicity, are primarily assigned. But whether a cultural community is one we are born into or adopt, it is clear that not all of our cultural ties are equally important, equally salient, or equally influential across situations and across time. What the literature suggests, according to Frable (1997, p. 155), is that "the personal meanings of social group memberships change over time, and the meanings are best understood in the context of socio-historical events."

Thus, gender may trump ethnicity or sexual identity, or the latter may trump the former, at different times and in different places. In addition, for a particular person, a particular social identity may be relatively insignificant most of the time, since not all group memberships are equally valued and the same group membership will have varied meanings to different people. Over and above these considerations, for a particular person, a change in situation may evoke a particular cultural identity, or enhance or reduce its salience. One 1990 study by Luborsky and Rubenstein (cited in Tsai, Chentsova-Dutton & Wong, 2002) found, among a sample of Irish, Italian, and Jewish widowers, that their ethnic identity became more salient after the death of their wives. This enhanced their ability to retain connections with their earlier experiences and to assume their roles as cultural transmitters. Shelton and Sellers (2000) report data gathered with a sample of African American college students that indicated the increased importance of ethnicity in race-salient situations. They also found that the likelihood of interpreting an ambiguous event in terms of ethnicity increased with the importance or centrality of ethnic identification.

Roccas and Brewer (2002) present the example of a woman attorney. In some groups we expect her professional identity to be primary; in others, her gender. One of my daughters is an attorney and I have no doubt that when she appears to plead a case in court, it is the culture of the lawyer that is overwhelmingly (if not totally) influential in affecting her language and behavior. But, as Roccas and Brewer, note, "both gender and occupation may be equally salient in a work context" (p. 90), as was certainly the case when my daughter faced the difficult choice of staying home with a sick child when her daughter was younger or reporting for work and traveling to her office. Worchel (1999) notes that the salience of a particular identity may well change in response to a personal crisis. It may also be affected by a crisis for the cultural community. A racist, sexist, anti-Semitic, or heterosexist event, or series of events, in one's neighborhood or workplace or city may turn a relatively dormant or low-strength identity into one with far greater salience.

Situational cues play an essential role in making a particular social identity salient but cultural memberships are not all of equal strength. Tsai et al. (2000, p. 57) note that the degree to which "one feels oriented to Chinese culture may depend on whether one is speaking Chinese or English ..., or whether one is in the presence of an authority figure or peer." Ethier and Deaux (1994, p. 243) report having found, in a one-year longitudinal study of Latino/a students at a primarily Anglo college, that the strength of a studenrt's ethnic identity varied with "the language spoken in the home, the ethnic composition of the neighborhood, and the percentage of a student's friends who were in the same ethnic group." At the college, students with a stronger ethnic identity were more likely to get involved with other Latino/a students in cultural activities.

Even though socioeconomic status is powerfully linked to so many areas of life (health, education, opportunities, privilege, material advantages), the meaningfulness of one's social class will vary greatly across persons and across situations (Liu, 2001). It is particularly difficult in the United States, where the myth of classlessness is still strong, for working-class or low-income persons to claim this identity despite awareness of economic and sociopolitical inequities. Fine and Burns (2003, p. 855) point out that

> [T]here is little pride in being poor or working class ... it is just assumed that it is 'better' to be middle- or upper-middle-class.... The desire to exit or be in the closet about poverty or the working class is understood.

Upward mobility is part of the American Dream (Ostrove & Cole, 2003), and being low-income is not a status to which anyone aspires. Positive stories about dignified and decent lives in working-class culture are infrequent in any of the mass media. Exceptions – films like *Norma Rae* (about textile mill workers) or *North Country* (about coal miners) – are notable by their small numbers. Depictions are more likely to be of dysfunctional, problematic families although, as hooks (2000, p. 72) notes, "On television the working class are allowed to be funny now and then." Most often, it is affluence that is pictured as better, superior, and to be admired and strived for. Wealth is deserved and earned. Frable (1997) concluded, from a review of the empirical literature, that social class tends to become salient when an individual is in a clearly other-class context or situation – a working class student in an ivy-league school, a newly divorced middle-class woman experiencing a serious economic downturn, and so on.

There was a time in U.S. history when pride in union membership and working-class status was greater than it is now. I am old enough to remember the image of Rosie the Riveter who represented the army of proud working-class women who made enormous contributions to ending World War II by welding, hammering, and painting in factories and shipyards across the United States. These working women came from all over the U.S. "including...from states where blacks and whites wouldn't be sharing drinking fountains for another 20 years" (Locke, 2007, p. A2). I am also old enough to remember exuberant May Day marches down Fifth Avenue in New York City, equivalent in spirit to Gay Pride parades and to the Black is Beautiful movement. Union culture contained music, stories, and shared experiences that were passed down from one generation to another. But that culture now continues strong only in some regions of the U.S. and is a dominant identity for a small minority.

> Today ... the American union movement is a shadow of its former self, except among government workers [and some others]. In 1973, almost a quarter of private sector employees were union members ... [compared with today's] mere 7.4 percent (Krugman (2007, para. 2).

According to the Bureau of Labor Statistics, the total current union membership figure, including both government and private sector workers, is 12.1 percent of the workforce (cf. Zipperer & Schmitt,

2007). What has happened to the U.S. labor movement is largely the result of a concerted and powerful effort by corporate business to undermine and seriously injure it through both legal and illegal strategies. Anti-union campaigns against organizing efforts are run by law firms and consulting groups hired by 75 percent of employers; and a quarter of such employers illegally fire workers for union advocacy (Eiding & Slack, 2007). This determined corporate effort is in sharp contrast with the results of polls of non-managerial workers, half of whom express a desire for union membership (Zipperer & Schmitt, 2007); "close to 60 million workers say that they would join a union right now if given the opportunity to do so in a fair environment" (Eiding & Slack, 2007). Some note the success of the Service Employees International Union in reversing the decline of organized labor, and attribute this to its aggressive recruitment of minorities of color, and of the lowest paid service workers like home health workers and janitors (Keen, 2007). Recent gains in union membership generally are attributed to women and Black men (Zipperer & Schmitt, 2007).

Conflicting Identities

Special problems arise for persons in cultures with conflicting beliefs and values, and opposing behavioral prescriptions and proscriptions. Much has been written of clashes between ethnic identities and sexual minority identity (e.g., Greene, 2007; Harper, 2007). Allman (1996) notes that Asian Americans who are gay or lesbian may be chastised within their ethnic communities because homosexuality is considered to be a White problem/issue. At the same time, as a lesbian, she has experienced pressures to behave in accord with an unspoken lesbian norm of whiteness. Individual conflict resolution may involve attempts to integrate differences or to shift between cultures as the salience of each becomes more relevant in one situation or another. An African American gay man may be strongly connected to both Black and gay cultures. He may choose to be not "very public with his gay identity with his family or within his church" and yet not be closeted; at other times, he may associate "with predominantly White gay friends" and yet not be denying his African American culture (Reynolds & Pope, 1991, p. 178).

Anita Hill's testimony before the Senate committee reviewing the suitability of Clarence Thomas for membership on the U.S. Supreme

Court is a well-known example. Jordan (1995, p. 40) has discussed this event in the context of a clash of cultures – gender and ethnicity. "[O]ne of the ironclad conventions of black cultural life," she notes, is that you "Don't 'air our dirty laundry' in public" (p. 40). Hill's decision to speak out publicly as a Black woman who had experienced harassment from a Black man broke the "dirty linen" taboo. This made her vulnerable to criticism from within the African American community while being praised and receiving positive recognition from feminists. Purdie-Vaughns and Eibach (2008) provide an insightful discussion of the negative reception among some African Americans to Anita Hill's decision to make public her harassment charges against Thomas and the questions raised about why she waited so long to do so. Hill's hesitation is explained by the "norms within the black community which impose a 'code of silence' on black women" (p. 387), as evidenced by criticism in some of the Black media leveled against Hill for violating the taboo.

Cultural Intersections

Recognition of one's personal multiculturality can enhance awareness and widen one's sphere of action. Duberman (2001) urges greater understanding of the intersections among sexuality, social class, ethnicity and gender. Issues associated with each need to be listened to carefully so that we will be better informed about the similarities in "hierarchies of privilege and power" and have a more accurate picture of "the complexities and sometimes overlapping identities of individual lives" (p. 21). Providing a personal example of a complex life, Kich (1996) describes how being biracial and bisexual helped him to better appreciate the wide array of experiences and knowledge associated with ethnic and sexual marginality. Such analyses can encourage intercultural competence and aid in bridging and reconciling differences.

An *intersectionality* perspective is entering more and more frequently into theoretical discussions. This perspective acknowledges simultaneous, intersecting memberships in multiple social groups (Brewer & Pierce, 2005), and recognizes and highlights "the mutually constitutive relations among social identities" (Warner, 2008, p. 454). What is emphasized is that these do not function independently but interact to influence self-view and behavior.

Overlapping identities can be brought to the center of experience by reactions from others. Cose (1993) interviewed a sample of affluent Black professionals who reported incident after incident in which the White people with whom they were interacting were responding to their ethnicity and not to their social class or occupational and educational status. They reported humiliating experiences in which they were treated with disrespect and lack of acknowledgement of their capabilities and accomplishments. Other middle-class people of color have frequently reported such experiences. Hooks (2000) notes that the only cultural identity that seems to matter to store clerks, for example, is ethnicity.

To date, most of the theoretical and empirical work on intersectionality has focused on "people with multiple subordinate identities" (Purdie-Vayghns & Eibach, 2008, p. 378) in an effort to understand the effects of cumulative disadvantage. Hurtado and Sinha (2008) note that this concept was proposed by feminist scholars in reaction to a focus on women's oppression without consideration of social class, ethnicity, sexual identity, and other subordinate categories. But, to be maximally useful as a theoretical construct, intersectionality should be extended beyond such categories to understand the intersections among all the communities of which an individual is a part. Diamond and Butterworth (2008, p. 366) articulate such a broader view, defining intersectionality "as a framework for analyzing the way in which multiple social locations and identities mutually inform and constitute one another." These locations may vary in power, providing different degrees of access to resources.

Multiethnic writers have begun to share their experiences, challenges, and resolutions in fiction and memoirs (cf. Cardwell, 1998; Obama, 1995). Within psychology, there is a growing focus on biracial or mixed-ethnicity experiences (e.g., Root, 1990) and how those with a mixed ethnic heritage understand and define their identity. Reynolds and Pope (1991) assert that a resolution is necessary to allow for the coexistence of diverse parts of one's heritage. One possible resolution is identification with each, accompanied by understanding each in the context of oppression. The experience of restricted access to resources needed for optimum human development may serve as a bridge connecting membership in one minority culture with membership in another. Petersen (2006) illustrates this in presenting the experiences of an African American adult woman with disabilities. Recognition of her multiple identities encouraged a comprehensive and authentic understanding of her life.

Since there are "power relations associated with our multiple identities" (McDowell & Fang, 2007, p. 550), there will be significant variation across persons, times, and conditions in the degree to which identities are compatible or in opposition. Constructive recognition of them must be accompanied by an assessment of the differences that may exist among them in status and privilege and the extent to which each assists or obstructs our access to resources (Chisholm & Greeene. 2008). While one cultural community of which we are a part may put us in the majority and provide advantages (as with skin color, sexual orientation, gender, or religion), another may put us in a stigmatized or oppressed or disrespected minority. As yet, we seem to know little about the psychological consequences of such a state of affairs, about the situations or circumstances which result in disparate behavioral pulls or objectives coming from different cultural attachments, and about modes of reconciling them.

While a full understanding of individual experience requires seeing a whole person as more than the sum of discrete social identities or cultural memberships and recognizing their interdependence (Bowleg, 2008), it is very likely that different contexts can raise one membership to greater salience over others. The context can be seen to influence experience in a study of Caribbean American working-class persons (Mattis, Grayman, Cowie, Winston, Watson & Jackson, 2008). In a predominantly African American community, respondents felt their ethnicity to be most salient, but in a middle-class White community, what was most salient was social class.

Each cultural identity will be an influence on behavior to an extent that varies with context, situation, place, time, and expected consequences – sometimes presenting conflicting pressures and sometimes concordant ones, but always in interaction. And this interaction among multiple cultural memberships affects how people live, their vulnerabilities, and strengths and motivations. As noted by Shields (2008, p. 304), "Intersectionality first and foremost reflects the reality of lives." In giving full recognition to the intersectional consequences of multiple identities, we must also recognize at the same time that while "the salience, meanings, and functions of ... identities can change," as they are affected by national, institutional, personal, and geographic settings, some may be more likely to "remain fixed across time and across contexts" (Mattis, Grayman, Cowie, Winston & Watson, 2008, p. 426).

I finished writing this chapter soon after the election of Senator Barack Obama to the presidency of the United States. For some who worked hard for his election or just gave him their vote, it was the salience of ethnicity that mattered most; for many others, political culture values surpassed all others in importance. Personal behavior associated with the presidential candidacy of Obama illustrates the significance of ethnicity as a bond among African Americans. Black Americans differing in gender, sexual identity, and social class gave him an overwhelming level of support. At the same time, however, political values may trump ethnic bonds, and some influential Black voices were critical of Obama, even before he was inaugurated, for not being sufficiently focused on and not sharply articulating, problems stemming from racism and inequality (e.g., Muwakkil, 2008; Washington, 2008).

8

Some Implications for Research and Practice

[C]ultural meanings, practices, norms, and social institutions ... constitute the matrix in which are embedded the intentions, rules, practices, and activities through which people live their lives (Fiske, Kitayama, Markus & Nisbett, 1998, p. 917).

What goals or objectives must our profession and society adopt to become truly multicultural in vision, values, and practice? (Sue, Bingham, Porche-Burke & Vasquez, 1999, p. 1067).

This final chapter is the most difficult one to write. The quotations above suggest the complexity of understanding individual behavior within a cultural matrix. With the broad definition of culture proposed in this book, applicable to all significant groups that meet the criteria, complexity increases. To take seriously the multicultural nature of persons is to raise theoretical and empirical questions that are very difficult to answer. As a science and profession, we are not accustomed to thinking routinely and easily of individuals in this way. Our discipline will be enriched, however, if we can design creative new research strategies to address these questions.

The implications for practice may be least problematic because, whether in counseling, therapy, or education, theoretical emphasis has long been on taking into account "the whole person." And in these areas, there is typically one-on-one interaction between persons – between client and mental health worker, or between student and teacher. An individual's unique social identities or cultural memberships will be evident in behavior – overt or subtle. Whether they are recognized, acknowledged, respected and used positively in the actual *practice* of counseling, therapy, or education (beyond statements of theory) is a central concern. In research, a multicultural perspective presents a different set of interrelated problems pertaining to sampling, study design, methods, data analysis and interpretation.

Research

Each participant or respondent in an investigation brings to it unique experiences and beliefs, perceptions, and response potentials that reflect far greater individual complexity and far more cultural memberships than most researchers are prepared to identify. We agree with Shields (2008, p. 304) that "[t]he facts of our lives reveal that there is no single identity category that satisfactorily describes how we respond to our social environment or are responded to by others." We also agree with Mann and Kelley (1997, p. 392) that "knowledge is and should be situated in people's diverse social locations.... [and] grounded in the social biography of ... the observed." Such agreement, however, does not lead easily or directly to researchable empirical questions that can be investigated in a practical way. Multiple issues and problems face the researcher who is accustomed to obtaining demographic descriptions of participants that are usually limited to age, ethnicity, and gender, or to the single-identity or group-membership category viewed as an independent variable.

A viable strategy is to begin, first, with a stringent analysis of the dependent variable(s) under investigation. Suppose, for example, we are investigating the voting choice made in the 2008 presidential election. As West and Fenstermaker (1996) caution, gender, ethnicity, and social class are only three ways of exploring difference in social life. Beyond these are the possible influences of respondents' age, political culture, geography, family status, and other social identities found to be important in prior research on voting behavior. Instead of treating each of these as separable independent variables, a bundling approach may be more revealing and thus yield more accurate and reliable information. As noted by Frable (1997, p. 154) most research "focuses on the personal meanings of these social categories one at a time." But a politically conservative middle-aged middle-class gay Latino man living in Florida, for example, may behave in a way that reflects more than the sum of his individual identities.

I have no easy answer to the question posed by Shields (2008, p. 310) about how to "formulate research questions that allow for and can reveal the responses of individuals as a reflection of the identities that form them." I am, convinced, however, that we must collectively make the effort to devise and propose various possibilities. We will have to construct strategies for empirical research that will reveal the salience and influence of diverse cultural memberships and how they operate simultaneously in intersection (West & Fenstermaker, 1996). This will probably mean giving more careful attention to the design and analysis of qualitative studies.

In everyday interactions we are often surprised when persons do not behave as we assume or expect prototypical members of their cultures to act. One study by Mendes and colleagues found more than just surprise, but anxiety and defensive behavior, when participants were introduced to partners who were Asian American and spoke with southern drawls (cf. Munsey, 2007). Similarly, we may know that African American culture is not monolithic (Asumah & Perkins, 2000) but Black Republicans are disorienting. So are gay ("log cabin") Republicans, and so are women who choose not to bear or rear children, or American Indians who are not environmentalists. Researchers must move well beyond accepted assumptions in the investigations we design and the information we hope to obtain. For example, Akom (2000) describes a subset of urban inner-city African Americans for whom identity is *ghettocentric* and tied to the 'hood, not just to skin color. What matters most to them is experience, social class, and neighborhood. To organize research data around ethnicity without understanding such within-group variations and taking them into account will yield faulty or incomplete or inadequate information of little predictive value.

Warner (2008) cautions that explicit care be taken in choosing those categories of identity on which the research questions are best focused and *also* in choosing which are to be collapsed or ignored. These decisions will be influenced by theoretical concerns, by new hypotheses, and prior research. The new formulations which can guide research may well come from critical theory which posits that we all are embedded in a system of power relations. Thus, the politically conservative middle-aged middle-class gay Latino voter mentioned earlier is both advantaged (by gender and social class) and disadvantaged (by minority ethnicity and sexual identity) in comparison with others in his immediate and distant environment. Questions posed to study participants about their perceptions of such power considerations in relation to the realities of their daily lives may add considerably to the predictive utility of an investigation's findings.

Qualitative research and case studies may be more amenable to capturing the influence of multiple cultural memberships on behavior than the traditional quantitative research of experiments and surveys. But while the former are more likely to encourage respondents to reveal more of their complex and unique wholeness, the qualitative researcher, too, may not tap into the cultural communities that are most important to the research participant, or most relevant to the research question, by not asking the right questions. For example, a heterosexual African American woman who is part of a study about religion and spirituality may not ever be asked about the importance to her life of her single, never-married status. Bowleg (2008) has written convincingly about the difficulties facing qualitative researchers in attempting to capture the nuances of intersectionality, "the interdependence and mutuality of identities" (p. 316).

Practice

The avowed aim of counseling or psychotherapy is to assist individuals in coping constructively with the problems of living that are specific to their situations. This must surely necessitate recognizing an individual's multicultural uniqueness and understanding how particular social identities intersect in the past and present contexts that are relevant to the person. An explicitly multicultural training program (Dana, Gamst & Der-Karabetian, 2008) goes beyond attention to ethnicity. It calls for "recognition of the full array of possible identity components" (p. 293) and suggests that they and their interrelations function as positive sources of strength and power.

A "cultural context" model in clinical psychology, described by Hernandez (2008) suggests, further, that it is important to take into account the structural issues in society, to identify "the current and historical impact of oppressive social forces" (p. 10) that have impacted a client's experiences. An attempt to link interpersonal processes to larger societal institutions is seen as a goal of the therapeutic practice.

Similarly, Reid and Comas-Diaz (1990) call attention to the role of social status in mediating information and providing expectations to individuals and to those with whom they interact. "High status individuals are accepted as leaders and models; low status people are devalued and ignored" (p. 398). The personal and social consequences of status need to be recognized and taken into account in therapeutic practice. But status is not fixed. It can change with time, changed life circumstances, and situation. As Hurtado (1996, p. xii) has noted, "within certain contexts we can be victims of subordination, and within others we can be oppressors."

Seligman and Csikszentmihalyi (2001), in responding to criticism of work on "positive psychology" that has ignored people of color, maintain that positive psychological goals "cut across social and cultural divides" (p. 90). But such a hypothesis requires considerable testing before it can be accepted as a valid generalization. While it is likely that most cultures contain ideas and prescriptions about what is good and what is moral and acceptable behavior (Fiske, Kitayama, Markus & Nisbett, 1998), the content of these ideas and the direction of the prescriptions are known to vary. Individual striving for material success may well be considered a positive goal to strive for within some cultural communities, while cooperative efforts toward mutual benefits are positive goals within others. Similarly, developing one's physical strength to the maximum may not be a goal shared by those who prefer focusing on the development of their social or intellectual skills.

Assumptions about positive goals cannot be made within a counseling or clinical setting without considering social status and all the cultural memberships or identities that are most relevant and most salient. An emphasis on personal change may raise questions about maintaining or abandoning old goals and perhaps adopting others. But these goals are embedded in intersecting multicultural positions and cannot be easily understood without taking them into account.

What Now?

Pedersen (1999, p. 13) recognized the "profound consequences" for our discipline that arise from a "culture centered perspective." Others, cited throughout the pages of this book, have shared this recognition.

We will need to ask new research questions, formulate different hypotheses from those tested in the past, perhaps sample smaller populations, be much more sensitive to environments and to time and place and context. In assessment, formulation of generalizations, and proposing solutions to social and individual problems, we will need to consider as much as possible the multicultural nature of persons. Flannery, Reise, and Yu (2001), for example, make the case for emerging ethnicities and point to the uniqueness of Italian Americans living in New York City or Chinese Americans in San Francisco, Irish Americans in Boston, or Chicanos in Los Angeles.

Questions focused on ethnicity or gender or social class need to be reformulated so that these identities in combination are seen as more reliable predictors of different forms and different levels of social or political action. Under what conditions, if any, for example, will low-income heterosexual White urban men behave or react like middle-income African American women? The majority of both groups voted for Obama for president. What research would have led to this prediction? What strategies to increase union membership will be most effective with middle-aged Latinas, older Southern White men, young Midwestern white collar workers? How will the strategies differ or be much the same?

The newest mission statement for the American Psychological Association, adopted by the Council of Representatives (Farberman, 2008), speaks of advancing "the creation, communication, and application of psychological knowledge to benefit society and improve people's lives" (p. 70). To realize these objectives, we will need to do the best we can in searching for generalizations across persons and across cultures. Generality across settings, times, and populations, however, cannot be assumed (Tebes, 2000). We may well find an "essential sameness" among human beings" (Guyll & Madon, 2000, p. 1510) in capacities and needs. But when we study attitudes, beliefs, skills, values, social perceptions, and expectations, we will inevitably be compelled to respect and understand diversity and the multicultural uniqueness of individual persons.

References

Abes, E. S., & Kasch, D. (2007). Using queer theory to explore lesbian college students' multiple dimensions of identity. *Journal of College Student Development, 48,* 619–636.

Adair, V. C. (2005). The missing story of ourselves: Poverty class in academe. *Labor Studies in Working-Class History of the Americas, 2,* 33–47.

Adamopoulos, J., & Lonner, W. J. (2001). Culture and psychology at a crossroad. In D. Matsumoto (Ed.) *The handbook of culture and psychology* (pp. 11–34). New York: Oxford University Press.

Addis, M. E., & Cohane, G. H. (2005). Social scientific paradigms of masculinity and their implications for research and practice in men's mental health. *Journal of Clinical Psychology, 61,* 633–647.

Aizenman, N. C. (2008, February 12). Study finds America is again becoming a land of immigrants. *The Providence Journal,* p. A1.

Akom, A. A. (2000). The house that race built: Some observations on the use of the word *Nigga,* popular culture, and urban adolescent behavior. In L. Weis & M. Fine (Eds.), *Construction sites: Excavating race, class, and gender among urban youth* (pp. 140–157). New York: Teachers College Press.

Alaska's uniqueness helped shape, define Palin. (2008, September 4). *The Providence Journal,* p. A11.

Albright concludes she was born Jewish (1995, February 4). *The Providence Journal,* p. A3.

Alexander, J., & Yescavage, K. (2003). Introduction. In J. Alexander & K. Yescavage (Eds.), *Bisexuality and transgenderism: InterSEXions of the others* (pp. 3–23). Binghamton, NY: Harrington Park Press.

Allen, T. J. (2007, June). America's child soldier problem. *In These Times,* p. 45.

Allman, K. M. (1996). (Un)natural boundaries: Mixed race, gender and sexuality. In M. P. P. Root (Ed.), *The multiracial experience: Racial borders as the new frontier* (pp. 277–290). Thousand Oaks, CA: Sage.

Alvarez, J. (1991). *How the Garcia girls lost their accents*. Chapel Hill, NC: Algonquin Books.

Alvarez, J. (2007). *Once upon a quinceanera: Coming of age in the USA*. New York: Viking.

American Anthropological Association. (1997, September). *Response to OMB Directive 15: Race and ethnic standards for federal statistics and administrative reporting*. Available: http://www.aaanet.org/gvt/ombdraft.htm

American Psychological Association (APA). (2000). Guidelines for psychotherapy with lesbian, gay, and bisexual clients. *American Psychologist, 55*, 1440–1451.

American Psychological Association (APA). (2003). Guidelines on multicultural education, training, research, practice, and organizational change for psychologists. *American Psychologist, 58*, 377–402.

American Psychological Association (APA). (2007). Guidelines for psychological practice with girls and women. *American Psychologist, 62*, 949–979.

An anthem of hope, a legacy of pride. (1999, February 14). *New York Times*, p. 34 AR.

APA resolves to play leading role in improving treatment for gender-variant people. *APA Online*. Available: http://www.apa.org/releases/genderCO8.html

Aparicio, F. R. (2003). Jennifer as Selena: Rethinking Latinidad in media and popular culture. *Latino Studies, 1*, 90–105.

Aratani, L. (2008, February 10). Girls on equal footing with boys – buzz and all. *The Providence Journal*, p. A1.

Aries, E., & Seider, M. (2007). The role of social class in the formation of identity: A study of public and elite private college students. *Journal of Social Psychology, 147*, 137–157.

Arnett, J. J. (2002). The psychology of globalization. *American Psychologist, 57*, 774–783.

Aronson, P. (2008). The markers and meanings of growing up: Contemporary young women's transition from adolescence to adulthood. *Gender & Society, 22*, 56–82.

Asante, M. K. (1996, May–June). Multiculturalism and the academy. *Academe*, 20–23.

Associated Press (2008, November 15). Election spurs 'hundreds' of race threats, crimes. *USA Today*. Available: http://www.usatoday.com.news/politics/2008-11-15-obama-election-race_N/htm

Asumah, S. N., & Perkins, V. C. (2000). Black conservatism and the social problems in Black America: Ideological cul-de-sacs. *Journal of Black Studies, 31*, 51–73.

Atkins, D. (2003). (Ed). *Bisexual women in the twenty-first century*. New York: Haworth.

Austria, A. M. (2003). People of Asian descent: Beyond myths and stereotypes. In J. D. Robinson & L. C. James (Eds.), *Diversity in human interactions: The tapestry of America* (pp. 63–75). New York: Oxford University Press.

Auwarter, A. E., & Aruguete, M. S. (2008). Effects of student gender and socioeconomic status on teacher perceptions. *Journal of Educational Research, 101,* 243–246.

Bai, M. (2008, August 10). What would a black president mean for black politics? *The New York Times Magazine,* 34–41, 50, 54–55.

Baldwin, J. W., Faulkner, S. L., Hecht, M. L., & Lindsley, S. L. (Eds.). (2006). *Redefining culture: Perspectives across the disciplines.* Mahwah, NJ: Lawrence Erlbaum.

Barber, C. (2008, February 10). Healing a troubled mind takes more than a pill. *The New York Times,* p. B01.

Barry, R. (2000). Sheltered 'children': The self-creation of a safe space by gay, lesbian, and bisexual students. In L. Weis. & M. Fine (Eds.), *Consruction sites: Excavating race, class, and gender among urban youth* (pp. 84–99). New York: Teachers College Press.

Beckenroth-Ohsako, G. A. M. (1999). Multiculturalism and the deaf community: Examples given from deaf people working in bicultural groups. In P. Pedersen (Ed.), *Multiculturalism as a fourth force* (pp. 111–146). Philadelphia: Bruner/Mazel.

Begley, S. (2004, October 29). Ancestry trumps race in predicting efficacy of drug treatments. *Wall Street Journal,* p. B1.

Belkin, L. (2008, June 15). When mom and dad share it all. *The New York Times Magazine,* 44–51, 74, 78.

Bell, D. (1997, June 17). Let's study the effect of racism on whites. *Providence Journal Bulletin,* p. B7.

Bento, R. F. (1997). When good intentions are not enough: Unintentional subtle discrimination against Latinas in the workplace. In N. V. Benokraitis (Ed.), *Subtle sexism: Current practice and prospects for change* (pp. 95–116). Thousand Oaks, CA: Sage.

Bergerson, A. A. (2007). Exploring the impact of social class on adjustment to college: Anna's story. *International Journal of Qualitative Studies in Education, 20,* 99–119.

Bernhardt, A. (2007, July 9). What we owe the working poor. *The Nation.* Available: http://www.thenation.com/doc/20070716/bernhardt.

Berry, J. W., & Poortinga, Y. H. (2006). Cross-cultural theory and methodology. In J. Georgas, J. W. Berry, F. J. R. van de Vijver, C. Kagitcibasi, & Y. H. Poortinga (Eds.), *Families across cultures: A 30-nation psychology study* (pp. 51–71). New York: Cambridge University Press.

Berube, A. (1997). Intellectual desire. In Raffo, S. (Ed.), *Queerly classed: Gay men and lesbians write about class* (pp. 43–66). Boston: South End Press.

Betancourt, H., & Fuentes, J. L. (2001). Culture and Latino issues in health psychology. In S. S. Kazarian & D. R. Evans (Eds.), *Handbook of cultural health psychology* (pp. 305–321). San Diego, CA: Academic Press.

Betancourt, H., & Lopez, S. R. (1993). The study of culture, ethnicity, and race in American psychology. *American Psychologist, 48*, 629–637.

Bettie, J. (2000). Women without class: Chicas, cholas, trash, and the presence/absence of class identity. *Signs, 26*, 1–36.

Bettie, J. (2003). *Women without class: Girls, race, and identity.* Berkeley, CA: University of California Press.

Bhatia, S., & Stam, H. J. (2005). Critical engagements with culture and self: Introduction. *Theory & Personality, 15*, 419–430.

Biale, D. (1988). The melting pot and beyond: Jews and the politics of American identity. In D. Biale, M. Galchinsky, & S. Heschel (Eds.), *Insider/outsider: American Jews and multiculturalism* (pp. 17–33). Berkeley, CA: University of California Press.

Biale, D., Galchinsky, M., & Heschel, S. (1988). The dialectic of Jewish enlightenment. In D. Biale, M. Galchinsky, & S. Heschel (Eds.), *Insider/ outsider: American Jews and multiculturalism* (pp. 1–13). Berkeley, CA: University of California Press.

Bloom, A. (2007). *Away.* New York: Random House.

Bloom, J. (2007). (Mis)reading social class in the journey towards college: Youth development in urban America. *Teachers College Record, 109*, 343–368.

Blumstein, P. W., & Schwartz, P. (1990). Intimate relationships and the creation of sexuality. In D. P. McWhirter, S. A. Sanders, & J. M. Reinisch (Eds.), *Homosexuality/heterosexuality: Concepts of sexual orientation* (pp. 307–320). New York: Oxford University Press.

Blumstein, P. W., & Schwartz, P. (2000). Bisexuality: Some social psychological issues. In P. C. R. Rust (Ed.), *Bisexuality in the United States* (pp. 339–351). New York: Columbia University Press.

Bond, M. H. (2004). Culture and aggression- from context to coercion. *Personality & Social Psychology Review, 8*, 62–78.

Boushey, H. (2007, September/October). Working family values. *Sojourner Magazine, 9*, 7.

Bousquet, D. (1997). *Don Bousquet's next book.* New York: Douglas Charles.

Bowleg, L. (2008). When Black + lesbian + woman ≠ Black lesbian woman: The methodological challenges of qualitative and quantitative intersectionality research. *Sex Roles, 59*, 312–325.

Boyarin, D., & Boyarin, J. (1997). So what's new? In J. Boyarin & D. Boyarin (Eds.), *Jews and other differences* (pp. vii–xxii). Minneapolis: University of Minnesota Press.

Boyd, R. S. (1996, November 28). Many scientists now reject the notion of separate races. *The Providence Journal-Bulletin*, p. F6.

Breines, J. G., Crocker, J., & Garcia, J. A. (2008). Self-identification and well-being in women's daily lives. *Personality & Social Psychology Bulletin, 34,* 583–598.

Brewer, M. B., & Pierce, K. P. (2005). Social identity complexity and out-group tolerance. *Personality & Social Psychology Bulletin, 31,* 428–437.

Brick, M. (2008, May 30). Ultimate fighting recruits military to its ranks. *The New York Times,* Available: http://www.nytimes.com/2008/05/30/sports/othersports/30fight.htm

Britzman, D. P. (1996). Difference in a minor key: Some modulations of history, memory, and community. In M. Fine, L. Weis, L. Powell, & L. M. Wong (Eds.), *Off White: Readings on race, power, and society* (pp. 29–39). New York: Routledge.

Brodkey, L. (2000). Writing on the bias. In L. Weis & M. Fine (Eds), *Construction sites: Excavating race, class, and gender among urban youth* (pp. 5–25). New York: Teachers College Press.

Brookings Institute (2006, July). *From poverty, opportunity.* Available: http://www.brookings.edu/metropubs/20060718_POVOP.htm

Brown, L. S. (1989). New voices, new visions: Toward a lesbian/gay paradigm for psychology. *Psychology of Women Quarterly, 13,* 445–458.

Browning, L. (2008, Aug. 13). Study tallies corporations not paying income tax. *The New York Times,* Available: http://www.nytimes.com/2008/08/13/business/13tax.htm

Brownworth, V. A. (1997). Life in the passing lane: Exposing the class closet. In Raffo, S. (Ed.), *Queerly classed: Gay men and lesbians write about class* (pp. 67–78). Boston: South End Press.

Bullock, H. E., & Lott, B. (2009). Social class and power. Unpublished MS.

Bullock, H. E., Lott, B., & Wyche, K. F. (2010). Making room at the table: Gender, ethnic and class inequities. In H. Landrine & N. Russo (Eds.), *Handbook of feminist psychology.* New York: Springer.

Burleson, B. R., & Kunkel, A. (2006). Revisiting the different cultures thesis: An assessment of sex differences and similarities in supportive communication. In K. Dindia & D. J. Canary (Eds.), *Sex differences and similarities in communication* (2nd ed.) (pp. 137–159). Mahwah, NJ: Lawrence Erlbaum.

Bynoe, Y. (2007, October 11). Presidential candidates ignore working mothers. *Alternet.* Available: http://www.alternet.org/story/64712/

Caldwell-Colbert, A. T., Henderson-Daniel, J., & Dudley-Grant, G. R. (2003). In J. D. Robinson & L. C. James (Eds.), *Diversity in human interactions: The tapestry of America* (pp. 33–61). New York: Oxford.

Cameron, D. (2007). *The myth of Mars and Venus: Do men and women really speak different languages?* New York: Oxford University Press.

Carbado, D. W. (2005). Privilege. In E. P. Johnson & M. G. Henderson (Eds.), *Black queer studies: A critical anthology* (pp. 190–212). Durham, NC: Duke University Press.

Cardwell, D. (1998, June 21). Crossing the great divide. *The New York Times Magazine,* p. 20.

Carter, R. T. (1997). Is White a race: Expressions of White racial identity. In M. Fine, L. Weis, L. Powell, & L. M. Wong (Eds.), *Off White: Readings on race, power, and society* (pp. 198–209). New York: Routledge.

Carter, S. L. (2007). *New England White.* New York: Knopf.

Caulkins, D. D. (2001). Consensus, clines, and edges in Celtic cultures. *Cross-Cultural Research, 35* (2), 109–126.

Cavanagh, J., & Collins, C. (2008, June 30). The rich and the rest of us. *The Nation,* pp. 11–12.

CDC. (2007). Cases of HIV infection and AIDS in the United States and dependent areas, 2005. Vol. 17 (revised). Atlanta, GA: US Department of Health and Human Services. Available: http://www.cdc.gov/hiv/topics/surveillance/resources/reports

Center on Budget and Policy Priorities (2007, August 31). *Number and percentage of Americans who are uninsured climbs again.* Available: www.cbpp.org/8-28-07pov.doc

Centrie, C. (2000). Free spaces unbound: Families, community, and Vietnamese high school students' identities. In L. Weis & M. Fine (Eds.), *Construction sites: Excavating race, class, and gender among urban youth* (pp. 65–83). New York: Teachers College Press.

Cervantes, J. M. (2006). A new understanding of the macho male image: Exploration of the Mexican American man. In M. Englar-Carlson & M. A. Stevens (Eds.), *In the room with men: A casebook of therapeutic change* (pp. 197–224). Washington, DC: American Psychological Association.

Champlin, D. P., & Knoedler, J. T. (2008). American prosperity and the "race to the bottom": Why won't the media ask the right questions? *Journal of Economic Issues, 42,* 133–151.

Chang, D. F., & Demyan, A. L. (2007). Teachers' stereotypes of Asian, Black, and White students. *School Psychology Quarterly, 22,* 91–114.

Chavez, D. (1994). *Face of an angel.* New York: Farrar, Straus, & Giroux.

Chin, J. L. (2000a). Asian American women: Many voices, different sounds. In J. L. Chin (Ed.), *Relationships among Asian American women* (pp. 5–12). Washington, DC: American Psychological Association.

Chin, J. L. (2000b). Paradigms for Asian American women: Power and connections. In J. L. Chin (Ed.), *Relationships among Asian American women* (pp. 223–230). Washington, DC: American Psychological Association.

Chisholm, J., & Greene, B. (2008). Women of color: Perspectives on "multiple identities" in psychological theory, research, and practice. In F. L. Denmark & M. A. Paludi (Eds.), *Psychology of women: A handbook of issues and theories* (2nd ed., pp. 40–69). Westport, CT: Praeger.

Christensen, K. (1997). With whom do you believe your lot is cast? White feminists and racism. *Signs, 22,* 617–648.

Chute, C. (1985). *The Beans of Egypt, Maine.* New York: Ticknor & Fields.

Clare, E. (1997). Losing home. In S. Raffo (Ed.), *Queerly classed: Gay men and lesbians write about class* (pp. 15–28). Boston: South End Press.

Clark, R., Anderson, N. B., Clark, V. R., & Williams, D. R. (1999). Racism as a stressor for African Americans: A biopsychosocial model. *American Psychologist, 54,* 805–816.

Clayton, S., & Opotow, S. (2003). Justice and identity: Changing perspectives on what is fair. *Personality & Social Psychology Review, 7,* 298–310.

Cohen, C. J. (2005). Punks, bulldaggers, and welfare queens: The radical potential of queer politics. In E. P. Johnson & M. G. Henderson (Eds.), *Black queer studies: A critical anthology* (pp. 21–51). Durham, NC: Duke University Press.

Cohen, D. (2001). Cultural variation: Considerations and implications. *Psychological Bulletin, 127* (4), 451–471.

Cohen, M. N. (1998). *Culture of intolerance.* New Haven, CT: Yale University Press.

Cole, S. (2000). Issues of transgender. In L. T. Szuchman & F. Muscarella (Eds.), *Psychological perspectives on human sexuality* (pp. 149–195). Hoboken, NJ: Wiley.

Conger, R. D., & Donnellan, M. B. (2007). An interactionist perspective on the socioeconomic context of human development. *Annual Reviews of Psychology, 58,* 175–199.

Coniff, R. (2006, March 23). Stop feeding the work monster. *The Progressive.* Available: http://www.progressive.org/mag-rcb032206.

Cooney, K. (2006). Mothers first, not work first: Listening to welfare clients in job training. *Qualitative Social Work, 5,* 217–235.

Corcoran, E. (2006, August 23). Counterpoint: Don't marry a lazy man. *Forbes.com.* Available: http://www.forbes.com/2006/08/23/Marriage-Careers-Divorce_cx_mn_land.htm

Cose, E. (1993). *The rage of a privileged class.* New York: Harper Collins.

Cramer, R. A. (2006). The common sense of anti-Indian racism: Reactions to Mashantucket Pequot success in gaming. *Law & Social Inquiry, 31,* 313–341.

Crary, D. (2008, February 28). Record-high ratio of Americans in prison. *Associated Press.* Available: http://urlet.com/intend.income

Crenshaw, K. W. (1992). Whose story is it anyway? Feminist and antiracist appropriations of Anita Hill. In T. Morrison (Ed.), *Race-ing justice, en-gendering power: Essays on Anita Hill, Clarence Thomas, and the construction of social reality* (pp. 402–440). New York: Knopf.

Cullum, J., & Harton, H. C. (2007). Cultural evolution: Interpersonal influence, issue importance, and the development of shared attitudes in college residence halls. *Personality & Social Psychology Bulletin, 33,* 1327–1339.

Dana, R. H., Gamst, G. C., & Der-Karabetian, A. (2008). *CBMCS Multicultural Training Program.* Thousand Oaks, CA: Sage.

Deaux, K. (2006). *To be an immigrant.* New York: Russell Sage.

Delbanco, A. (2007, September 30). Academic business. *The New York Times Magazine,* pp. 25–29.

Demos. (2008, February 21). Many African-American and Latina families in danger of falling out of middle-class. Available: http://www.demos.org

DeNavas-Walt, C., Proctor, B. D., Smith, J., & U.S. Census Bureau (2007, August). Income, poverty, and health insurance coverage in the United States: 2006. In *Current Population Reports* (pp. 60–233). Washington, DC: U.S. Government Printing Office.

Denison, D. (2008, March 9). Watching the rich give. *The New York Times Magazine,* p. 14.

Denmark, F. L., & Paludi, M. A. (Eds.). (2008). *Psychology of women: A handbook of issues and theories (second edition).* Westport, CT: Praeger.

Denner, J., & Guzman, B. L. (2006). Introduction: Latina girls transforming culture, contexts, and selves. In J. Denner & B. L. Guzman (Eds.), *Latina girls: Voices of adolescent strength in the United States* (pp. 1–14). New York: New York University Press.

DePaulo, B. (2006). *Singled out.* New York: St. Martin's Press.

Devine, P. G. (1989). Stereotypes and prejudice: Their automatic and controlled components. *Journal of Personality & Social Psychology, 56,* 5–18.

Diallo, D. D. (2008, May/June). HIV prevention and reproductive justice: A framework for saving women's lives. *The Women's Health Activist, 1,* 3–4, 7.

Diamond, L. M. (2003). Was it a phase? Young women's relinquishment of lesbian/bisexual identities over a 5-year period. *Journal of Personality & Social Psychology, 84,* 352–364.

Diamond, L. M. (2008). Female bisexuality from adolescence to adulthood: Results from a 10-year longitudinal study. *Developmental Psychology, 44,* 5–14.

Diamond, L. M., & Butterworth, M. (2008). Questioning gender and sexual identity: Dynamic links over time. *Sex Roles, 59,* 365–376.

Dottolo, A. L., & Stewart, A. J. (2008). "Don't ever forget now, You're a Black Man in America": Intersections of race, class and gender in encounters with the police. *Sex Roles, 59*, 350–364.

Downing, R. A., LaVeist, T. A., & Bullock, H. E. (2007). Intersections of ethnicity and social class in providing advice regarding reproductive health. *American Journal of Public Health, 97*, 1803–1807.

Duberman, M. (2001, July 9). In defense of identity politics. *In These Times*, pp. 20–21.

Duffy, J. (2007, September). Social class and higher education: The widening gaps in educational opportunities. *Class Action*. September 2007 E-news. Available: info@classism.org

Dunn, C. (2008, June 21). Living the high life in Providence. *The Providence Journal*, pp. A1, A5.

Eckhlolm, E. (2006a, July 19). Study documents 'ghetto tax' being paid by the urban poor. *The New York Times*, Available: http://www.nytimes.com/2006/07/19/us/19poor/html

Eckholm, E. (2006b, August 20). In rural Oregon, these are the times that try working people's hopes. *The New York Times*, p. YT12.

Eckholm, E. (2007, November 24). Barely getting by and facing a cold Maine winter. *The New York Times*. Available: http://www.nytimes.com/2007/11/24/us/24maine/html

Economic Policy Institute (2006). *The state of working America 2006/2007*. Available: http://www.stateofworkingamerica.org/swa06-ch05-wealth.pdf

Editorial (2008, June 12). The plight of the underinsured. *The New York Times*. Available: http://www.nytimes.com/2008/06/12/opinion/12thu2/html

Edney, H. T. (2007, September 18). African Americans remain at economic rock bottom. *New America Media*. Available: del.icio.us.

Ehrenreich, B. (1989). *Fear of falling: The inner life of the middle class*. New York: Pantheon.

Ehrenreich, B. (2008a, February 3). The boom was a bust for ordinary people. *The Washington Post*, p. BO1.

Ehrenreich, B. (2008b, June 30). This land is their land. *The Nation*, pp. 28–29.

Eiding, P., & Slack. E. (2007, December 20). Advancing workers' rights. *Philadephia Daily News*. Available: http://www.philly.com/dail/news/opinion/20071220_Advancing_workers_rights.html

Eisele, H., & Stake, J. (2008). The differential relationship of feminist attitudes and feminist identity to self-efficacy. *Psychology of Women Quarterly, 32*, 233–244.

Eligon, J. (2008, October 9). Young, Black, and Republican in New York, blogging against the tide. *The New York Times*, Available: http://www.nytimes.com/2008/10/09/nyregion/09repubblog.html

Endo, R. (1973). Whither ethnic studies: A re-examination of some issues. In S. Sue & N. N. Wagner (Eds.) *Asian-Americans: Psychological Perspectives* (pp. 281–294). Ben Lomond, CA: Science & Behavior Books.

Englar-Carlson, M. (2006). Masculine norms and the therapy process. In M. Englar-Carlson & M. A. Stevens (Eds.), *In the room with men* (pp. 13–47). Washington, DC: American Psychological Association.

Entman, R, M., & Rojecki, A. (2000). *The Black image in the White mind: Media and race in America.* Chicago: University of Chicago Press.

Erdrich, L. (1984). *Love medicine: A novel.* New York: Holt, Rinehart & Winston.

Erdrich, L. (1986). *The beet queen: A novel.* New York: Holt.

Erdrich, L. (2005). *The painted drum.* New York: Harper Collins.

Essed, P. (1996). *Diversity, gender, color, and culture.* Amherst. MA: University of Massachusetts Press.

Espiritu, Y. L. (1997). *Asian American women and men: Labor, law, and love.* Thousand Oaks, CA: Sage.

Ethier, K., & Deaux, K. (1994). Negotiating social identity when contexts change: Maintaining identification and responding to threat. *Journal of Personality & Social Psychology, 67,* 243–251.

Fallon, M. A., & Jome, L. M. (2007). An exploration of gender-role expectations and conflict among women rugby players. *Psychology of Women Quarterly, 31,* 311–321.

Farberman, R.K. (2008, October). A review of task force reports tops council's agenda. *Monitor on Psychology,* 68–70.

Fears D. (2003, August, 25). Latinos or Hispanics? A debate about identity. *The Washington Post,* p. AO1.

Feinstein, D. (2004). Personal reflection. In J. Pearl & R. Pearl (Eds.) *I am Jewish: Personal reflections inspired by the last words of Daniel Pearl* (pp. 228–229). Woodstock, VT: Jewish Lights Publishing.

Fenton, S. (1999). *Ethnicity: Racism, class and culture.* Lanham, MD: Rowman & Littlefield.

Feuer, A. (2008, October 7). Accommodations for the discreetly superrich. *The New York Times, p.,* A26.

Fine, M. (1997). Witnessing whiteness. In M. Fine, L. Weis, L.. Powell, & L. M. Wong (Eds.), *Off White: Readings on race, power, and society* (pp. 57–65). New York: Routledge.

Fine, M., & Burns, A. (2003). Class notes: Toward a critical psychology of class and schooling. *Journal of Social Issues, 59,* 841–860.

Fine, M., Burns, A., Payne, Y. A., & Torre, M. E. (2004). Civics lessons: The color and class of betrayal. *Teachers College Record, 106,* 2193–2223.

Fine, M., & Weis, L. (2003). (Eds.). *Silenced voices and extraordinary conversations: Re-imagining schools.* New York: Teachers College Press.

Fish, J. (1998, February). Ethnocentric ignorance. *APA Monitor*, 5.

Fiske, A. P., Kitayama, S., Markus, H. R., & Nisbett, R. E. (1998). The cultural matrix of social psychology. In D. Gilbert, S. Fiske, & B. Lindzey (Eds.), *Handbook of social psychology* (4th ed.) (pp. 915–981). New York: McGraw-Hill.

Flannery, W. P., Reise, S. P., & Yu, J. (2001). An empirical comparison of acculturation models. *Personality & Social Psychology Bulletin, 27,* 1035–1045.

Foley, D. E. (1997). Deficit thinking models based on culture: The anthropological protest. In R. R. Valencia (Ed.), *The evolution of deficit thinking: Educational thought and practise* (pp. 113–131). London: The Falmer Press.

Forman, J., & Giles, H. (2006). Communicating culture. In J. W. Baldwin, S. L. Faulkner, M. L. Hecht, & S. L. Lindsley (Eds.), *Redefining culture: Perspectives across the disciplines* (pp. 91–102). Mahwah, NJ: Lawrence Erlbaum.

Foster, D. (1997, January 27). Tribes ask: Who are the 'real' Indians? *The Providence Journal*, p. 43.

Fowers, B. J., & Davidow, B. J. (2006). The virtue of multiculturalism: Personal transformation, character, and openness to the other. *American Psychologist, 61,* 581–594.

Fowers, B. J., & Richardson, F. C. (1996). Why is multiculturalism good? *American Psychologist, 51,* 609–621.

Fox, D., & Prilleltensky, I. (Eds.). (1997). *Critical psychology: An introduction.* Thousand Oaks, CA: Sage.

Frable, D. E. (1997). Gender, racial, ethnic, sexual, and class identities. *Annual Review of Psychology, 48,* 139–163.

Frank, Reanne. (2007). What to make of it? The (Re)emergence of a biological conceptualization of race in health disparities research. *Social Science & Medicine, 64,* 1977–1983.

Frank Robert. (2007). *Richistan. A journey through the American wealth boom and the lives of the new rich.* New York: Crown.

Frazier, E. F. (1957). *Black bourgeoisie.* Glencoe, IL: Free Press.

Friedman, S. S. (1995). Beyond white and other: Relationality and narratives of race in feminist discourse. *Signs, 21 (1),* 1–49.

Gaines, S. O., Jr., & Reed, E. S. (1995). Prejudice: From Allport to DuBois. *American Psychologist, 50,* 96–103.

Garcia, C. (1992). *Dreaming in Cuban.* New York: Ballentine Books.

Garnets, L., & Kimmel, D. (1991). Lesbian and gay male dimensions in the psychological study of human diversity. In J. Goodchilds (Ed.), *Psychological perspectives on human diversity in America* (pp. 137–192). Washington, DC: American Psychological Association.

Gates, H. L. Jr. (2007, November 18). Forty acres and a gap in wealth. *The New York Times*, p. 14WK.

Gatewood, J. B. (2001). Reflections on the nature of cultural distributions and the units of culture problem. *Cross-Cultural Research, 35* (2), 227–241.

Gilbert, L. A. (1994). Reclaiming and returning gender to context: Examples from studies of heterosexual dual-earner families. *Psychology of Women Quarterly, 18,* 539–558.

Gillborn, D. (2006). Rethinking white supremacy: Who counts in 'White-World'. *Ethnicities, 6,* 318–340.

Gilman, S. L. (1991). *The Jew's body.* New York: Routledge.

Gilman, S. L. (1996). *Smart Jews: The construction of the image of Jewish superior intelligence.* Lincoln, NE: University of Nebraska Press.

Gitlitz, D. M. (1996). *Secrecy and deceit: The religion of the crypto Jews.* Philadelphia: Jewish Publication Society.

Ginwright, S. A. (2007). Black youth activism and the role of critical social capital in Black community organizations. *American Behavioral Scientist, 51,* 403–418.

Giroux, H. A. (1999). Rewriting the discourse of racial identity: Toward a pedagogy and politics of whiteness. In C. Clark & J. O'Donnell (Eds.), *Becoming and unbecoming White: Owning and disowning a racial identity* (pp. 224–252). Westport, CT: Bergin & Garvey.

Gladwell, M. (2007, December 17). None of the above: What IQ doesn't tell you about race. *The New Yorker.* Available: http://www.gladwell.com/2007/2007_12_17_e_iq.html

Glassgold, J. M., & Drescher, J. (Eds.). (2007). *Activism and LGBT psychology.* Binghamton, NY: Haworth.

Glater, J. D. (2008, June 2). Student loans start to bypass 2-year colleges. *The New York Times.* Available: http://www.nytimes.com/2008/06/02/business/02loans/html

Golden, C. (2009). The intersexed and the transgendered: Rethinking sex/gender. In J. W. White (Ed.), *Taking sides: Clashing views in gender* (4th edition, pp. 22–29). Boston: McGraw Hill.

Gonzalez, J. (2005, November 8). Racial divide evident in military. *New York Daily News.* Available: http://www.common dreams.org.views05/1108-29.htm.

Goodman, P. S. (2008, July 31). A hidden toll on employment: Cut to part time. *The New York Times,* Available: http://www.nytimes.com/2008/07/31/business/economy/31jobs.html

Goodsell, T. L. (2008). Diluting the cesspool: Families, home improvement, and social change. *Journal of Family Issues, 29,* 539–565.

Goodstein, L. (2003, October 8). A photographer's odyssey captures a myriad of identities. *The New York Times.* Available: http://www.nytimes.com/2003/10/08/arts/design/08BREN.html

Government Accountability Office (2007, January). *Poverty in America.* Available: www.gao.gov/cgi-bin/getrrpt?GAO-07-344

Graham, L. O. (1999). *Our kind of people: Inside America's black upper class.* New York: Harper Collins.

Gray, H. (2002, Spring). The Native American struggle: One century into another. *Democratic Left*, 8–11.

Green, A. I. (2007). On the horns of a dilemma: Institutional dimensions of the sexual career in a sample of middle-class, urban, Black, gay men. *Journal of Black Studies, 37*, 753–774.

Greene, B. (1994). Lesbian women of color. Triple jeopardy. In L. Comas-Diaz & B. Greene (Eds.), *Women of color: Integrating ethnic and gender identities in psychotherapy* (pp. 389–427). New York: Guilford.

Greene, B. (2003). Beyond heterosexism and across the cultural divide – Developing an inclusive lesbian, gay, and bisexual psychology: A look to the future. In L. D. Garnets & D. C. Kimmel (Eds.), *Psychological perspectives on lesbian, gay, and bisexual experiences* (2nd ed.) (pp. 357–400). New York: Columbia University Press.

Greene, B. (2007, August). Overview: Lesbians and gay men of color – Between the rock of ethnoracial identity and the hard place of heterosexism. *Communiqué*, iii–vii.

Grisham, J. (2008). *The appeal.* New York: Doubleday.

Guishard, M., Fine, M., Doyle, C., Jackson, J., Travis, S., & Webb, A. (2005). The Bronx on the move: Participatory consultation with mothers and youth. *Journal of Educational and Psychological Consultation, 16*, 35–54.

Guiso, L., Monte, F., Sapienza, P., & Zingales, L. (2008, May 30). Culture, gender, and math. *Science, 320*, 1164–1165.

Guyll, M., & Madon, S. (2000). Ethnicity research and theoretical conservatism. *American Psychologist, 55*, 1509–1510.

Hahn, C. (2006, Winter). Wanted: Women in the House (and Senate). *Ms*, 16.

Hahn, K. J. (2008). "Movin' on up": Different faces of upward mobility in an interracial couple. *St. Thomas Law Review, 20*, 495—502.

Haldeman, D. C., & Buhrke, R. A. (2003). Under the rainbow flag: The diversity of sexual orientation. In J. D. Robinson & L. C. James (Eds), *Diversity in human interactions: The tapestry of America* (pp. 145–156). New York: Oxford University Press.

Hall, G. C. N., & Barongan, C. (2000). *Multicultural psychology.* Upper Saddle River, NJ: Prentice Hall.

Hamill, J. F. (2003). Show me your CDIB: Blood quantum and Indian identity among Indian people of Oklahoma. *American Behavioral Scientist, 47*, 267–282.

Harmon, A. (2007, November 11). In DNA era, new worries about prejudice. *The New York Times*, p. YT1.

Harper, G. W. (2007). Sex isn't that simple: Culture and context in HIV prevention interventions for gay and bisexual male adolescents. *American Psychologist, 62,* 806–819.

Harper, G. W., Jamil, O. B., & Wilson, B. D. M. (2007). Collaborative community-based research as activism: Giving voice and hope to lesbian, gay, and bisexual youth. In J. M. Glassgold & J. Drescher (Eds.), *Activism and LGBT psychology* (pp. 99–119). Binghampton, NY: Haworth.

Harris. G. (2008, October 16). Infant deaths drop in U.S., but rate is still high. *The New York Times,* p. A19.

Haslam, N., Rothschild, L., & Ernst, D. (2000). Essentialist beliefs about social categories. *British Journal of Social Psychology, 39,* 113–127.

Haughney, C. & Konigsberg, E. (2008, April 14). Despite tough times, ultrarich keep spending. *The New York Times.* Available: http:www.nyt times.com/2008/04/14/nyregion/14partying.html

Hegarty, P., & Pratto, F. (2004). The differences that norms make: Empiricism, social constructivism, and the interpretation of group differences. *Sex Roles, 50,* 445–453.

Helms, J. E. (1994). The conceptualization of racial identity and other "racial" constructs. In E. J. Trickett, R. J. Watts, & D. Birman (Eds.), *Human diversity: Perspectives on people in context* (pp. 285–311). San Francisco: Jossey-Bass.

Helms, J. E., Jernigan, M., & Mascher, J. (2005). The meaning of race in psychology and how to change it: A methodological perspective. *American Psychologist, 60,* 27–36.

Herbert, B. (2007a, May 15). The right to paid sick days. *The New York Times.* Available: http://select.nytimes.com/2007/05/15/opinion/15herbert.html

Herbert, B. (2007b, June 2). Poisonous police behavior. *The New York Times.* Available: http://www.nytimes.com/2007/06/02/opinion/22herbert. html

Herbert, B. (2007c, July 14). Poor kids living in a war zone. *The New York Times.* Available: http://www.nytimes.com/2007/07/014/opinion/14herbert. html

Herbert, B. (2007d, December 22). Nightmare before Christmas. *The New York Times.* Available: http://www.nytimes.com/2007/12/22/opinion/ 22herbert.html

Herbert, B. (2008a, March 11). Sharing the pain. *The New York Times.* Available: http://www.nytimes.com/2008/03/11/opinion/11herbert. html

Herbert, B. (2008b, June 10). Out of sight. *The New York Times.* Available: http://www.nytimes.com/2008/06/10/opinion/10herbert.html

Herdt. G. (1997). *Same sex, different cultures: Gays and lesbians across cultures.* Boulder, CO: Westview Press.

Herek, G. M. (2003). Why tell if you're not asked? Self-disclosure, intergroup contact, and heterosexuals' attitudes toward lesbians and gay men. In L. D. Garnets & D. C. Kimmel (Eds.), *Psychological perspectives on lesbian, gay, and bisexual experiences* (2nd ed.) (pp. 270–298). New York: Columbia University Press.

Herek, G. M. (2007). Confronting sexual stigma and prejudice. *Journal of Social Issues, 63,* 905–925.

Herek, G. M., Kimmel, D. C., Amaro, H., & Melton, G. B. (1991). Avoiding heterosexist bias in psychological research. *American Psychologist, 46,* 957–963.

Hernandez, P. (2008). The cultural context model in clinical supervision. *Testing & Education in Professional Psychology, 2,* 10–17.

Hernstein, R. J., & Murray, C. (1996). *The bell curve: Intelligence and class structure in American life.* New York: Simon & Schuster.

Higgins, M. (2007, November 25). Aboard planes, class conflict. *The New York Times.* Available: http://travel.nytimes.com/2007/11/25/travel/25conflict.html

Hill, N. E., Murry, V. M., & Anderson, V. D. (2005). Socio-cultural contexts of African American families. In V. C. McLoyd, N. E. Hill, & K. A. Dodge (Eds.), *African American family life: Ecological and cultural diversity* (pp. 21–44). New York: Guilford.

Holmes, S. A. (2000, March 19). The politics of race and the census. *The New York Times,* p. WK 3.

Hong, Y-Y, Benet-Martinez, V., Chiu, C-Y, & Morris, M. W. (2003). Boundaries of cultural influence: Construct activation as a mechanism for cultural differences in social perception. *Journal of Cross-Cultural Psychology, 34,* 453–464.

Hong, Y-Y, Chan, G., Chiu, C-Y, Wong, R. Y. M., Hansen, I. G., Lee, S-L, Tong, Y-Y, & Ho-ying, F. (2003). How are social identities linked to self-conception and intergroup orientation? The moderating effect of implicit theories. *Journal of Personality & Social Psychology, 85,* 1147–1160.

Hong, Y-Y, Morris, M. W., Chiu, C-Y, & Benet-Martinez, V. (2000). Multicultural minds: A dynamic constructivist approach to culture and cognition. *American Psychologist, 55,* 709–720.

Hook, D., & Howarth, C. (2005). Future directions for a critical social psychology of racism/antiracism. *Journal of Community & Applied Social Psychology, 15,* 506–512.

hooks, b. (2000). *Where we stand: Class matters.* New York: Routledge.

Horsey (2008, March 17). Cartoon. *The Providence Journal,* p. C4.

Hotakainen, R. (2007, August 14). Half of nation's poor lack food stamps. *Providence Journal,* p. A4.

Howard, G. R. (1999). White man dancing: A story of personal transformation. In C. Clark & J. O'Donnell (Eds.), *Becoming and unbecoming White: Owning and disowning a racial identity* (pp. 212–223). Westport, CT: Greenwood.

Howard, J. A. (2000). Social psychology of identities. *Annual Review of Psychology, 26,* 367–393.

Hubbard, R. (1994). Race and sex as biological categories. In *Challenging racism and sexism* (pp. 11–21). New York: Feminist Press.

Huddy, L. (2001). From social to political identity: A critical examination of social identity theory. *Political Psychology, 22,* 127–156.

Hurtado, A. (1989). Relating to privilege: Seduction and rejection in the subordination of white women and women of color. *Signs, 14,* 833–855.

Hurtado, A. (1996). *The color of privilege: Three blasphemies on race and feminism.* Ann Arbor: University of Michigan Press.

Hurtado, A., & Sinha, M. (2008). More than men: Latino feminist masculinities and intersectionality. *Sex Roles, 59,* 337–349.

Hurtado, A., & Stewart, A. J. (1997). Through the looking glass. Implications of studying Whiteness for feminist methods. In M. Fine, L. Weis, L. Powell, & L. M. Wong (Eds.), *Off White: Readings on race, power, and society* (pp. 198–209). New York: Routledge.

Hyde, J. S. (2007, October). New directions in the study of gender similarities and differences. *Current Directions in Psychological Science, 16,* 259–263,

Hyde, J. S., Lindberg, S. M., Linn, M. C., Ellis. A. B., & Williams, C. C. (2008, July 25). Gender similarities characterize math performance. *Science, 321.*

Income needed to afford a home in R.I. (2006, May 17). *The Providence Journal,* p. A4.

Ip, G. (2007, October 12). Income-inequality gap widens. *The Wall Street Journal,* p. A2.

Ireland's Travelers seek recognition as an ethnic group. (2006, July 16). *The Providence Journal,* p. A8.

Itzkovitz, D. (1997). Secret temples. In J. Boyarin & D. Boyarin (Eds.), *Jews and other differences* (pp. 176–203). Minneapolis: University of Minnesota Press.

Jain, M. (2008, October 14). Equal treatment for the uninsured? Don't count on it. *The Washington Post,* p., HE05.

Jalata, A. (2002). Revisiting the Black struggle: Lessons for the 21st century. *Journal of Black Studies, 33,* 86–116.

Jencks, C. (1972). *Inequality: A reassessment of the effect of family and schooling in America.* New York: Basic Books.

Jennings, J. (2008, May 5). The Narragansetts: Indian race, culture and rights. *The Providence Journal,* p. C5.

Johnson, D. D., & Johnson, B. (2006). *High stakes: Poverty, testing, and failure in American schools.* Lanham, MD: Rowman & Littlefield.

Johnson, K. (2008, May 25). On the reservation and off, schools see a changing tide. *The New York Times.* Available: http:www.nytimes.com/2008/05/25/education/25hardin.html

Johnston, D. C. (2007a). *Free lunch: How the wealthiest Americans enrich themselves at government expense (and stick you with the bill).* New York: Portfolio.

Johnston, D. C. (2007b, May 29). Income gap is widening, data shows. *The New York Times,* Available: http:www.nytimes.com/2007/03/29/business/29tax.html

Jones, J. M. (1991). Psychological models of race: What have they been and what should they be? In J. D. Goodchilds (Ed.), *Psychological perspectives on human diversity in America* (pp. 3–46). Washington, DC: American Psychological Association.

Jones, J. M. (1998). Psychological knowledge and the new American dilemma of race. *Journal of Social Issues, 54,* 641–662.

Jones, S. (2007). Working-poor mothers and middle-class others: Psychosocial considerations in home-school relations and research. *Anthropology & Education Quarterly, 38,* 159–177.

Jones, S. J. (2003). Complex subjectivities: Class, ethnicity and race in women's narratives of upward mobility. *Journal of Social Issues, 59,* 803–820.

Jordan, E. C. (1995). The powers of false racial memory and the metaphor of lynching. In A. F. Hill & E. C. Jordan (Eds.), *Race, gender, and power in America* (pp. 37–55). New York: Oxford University Press.

Jost, L. J., & Jost, John T. (2007). Why Marx left philosophy for social science. *Theory & Psychology, 17*: 297–322.

Joyce, N., & Baker, D. B. (2008, May). Husbands, rate your wives. *Monitor on Psychology,* pp. 18–19.

Kakaiya, D. (2000). Identity development and conflict among Indian immigrant women. In J. L. Chin (Ed.), *Relationships among Asian American women* (pp.133–149). Washington, DC: American Psychological Association.

Kaplan, S. A., Calman, N. S., Golub, M., Davis, J. H., Ruddock, C., & Billings, J. (2006). Racial and ethnic disparities in health: A view from the South Bronx. *Journal of Health Care for the Poor & Underserved, 17,* 116–127.

Kaye/Kantrowitz, M. (2007). *The color of Jews: Racial politics and radical diasporism.* Bloomington: Indiana University Press.

Keen, C. (2007, December 19). UF researcher: Unions must recruit black in order to regain influence. *University of Florida News.* Available: http://news.ufl.edu/2007/12/19/unions/

Keita, M. (2002). Race, the writing of history, and culture wars. *Journal of Black Studies, 33,* 166–178.

Kich, G. K. (1996). In the margins of sex and race: Difference, marginality, and flexibility. In M. P. P. Root (Ed.), *The multiracial experience: Racial borders as the new frontier* (pp. 263–276). Thousand Oaks, CA: Sage.

Kim, J. L., Sorsoli, C. L., Collins, K., Zylbergold, B. A., Schooler, D., & Tolman, D. L. (2007). From sex to sexuality: Exploring the heterosexual script on primetime network television. *Journal of Sex Research, 44*, 145–157.

Kincheloe, J. L. (2004). Why a book on urban education? In S. R. Steinberg & J. L. Kincheloe (Eds.), *19 urban questions: Teaching in the city* (pp. 1–27). New York: P. Lang.

Kincheloe, J. L., & Steinberg, S. R. (2007). Cutting class in a dangerous era: A critical pedagogy of class awareness. In J. L. Kincheloe & S. R. Steinberg (Eds.), *Cutting class: Socioeconomic status and education* (pp. 3–69). Lanham, MD: Rowman & Littlefield.

King, E. W. (1997). Social class in the lives of young children: Cross cultural perspectives. *Education & Society, 15* (1), 3–12.

Kingston, M. H. (1976). *The woman warrior: Memoirs of a girlhood among ghosts.* New York: Alfred A. Knopf.

Kingston, M. H. (1980). *China men.* New York: Alfred A.Knopf.

Kitayama, D. (2002). Culture and basic psychological processes – Toward a system theory view of culture: Comment on Oyserman, et al. (2002). *Psychological Bulletin, 128*, 89–96.

Kitzinger, C. (1997). Lesbian and gay psychology: A critical analysis. In D. Fox & I. Prilleltensky (Eds.), *Critical psychology: An introduction* (pp. 202–216). Thousand Oaks, CA: Sage.

Knowles, D. (2008, November 13). Racists react to Obama victory. *AOL News.* Available: http://news.aol.com/political-machine/2008/11/13/shocker-racism-and-hatred-of-obama-stll-lives/

Koepping, G. R. (1996). The impact of economic disadvantage on gifted women's educational development. *Women & Therapy, 18*, 119–128.

Konigsberg, E. (2007, December 30). Never having to say, 'too expensive.' *The New York Times,* p. WK5.

Koppel, N. (2008, March 17). Black rabbi reaches out to mainstream of his faith. *The New York Times.* Available: http://www.nytimes.com/2008/03/16/us/16rabbi.html

Kranz, P. (2008, March 16). Measuring wealth by the foot. *The New York Times.* Available: http://www.nytimes.com/2008/03/16/business/16drop.html

Krech, S. III (1999). *The ecological Indian: Myth and history.* New York: W.W. Norton.

Kricorian, N. (2003). *Dreams of bread and fire.* New York. Grove Press.

Kroenke, C. (2008). Socioeconomic status and health: Youth development and neomaterialist and psychsocial mechanisms. *Social Science & Medicine, 66*, 32–42.

Krugman, P. (2006). *The great wealth transfer.* Available: http://www. informationclearinghouse.info/article15923.htm

Krugman, P. (2007, December 24). State of the Unions. *The New York Times.* Available: http://www.nytimes.com/2007/12/24/opinion/24krugman. html

Krugman, P. (2008, February 18). Poverty is poison. *The New York Times.* Available: http://www.nytimes.com/2008/02/18/opinion/ 18krugman.html

Laakso, J. H., & Drevedahl, D. J. (2006). Women, abuse, and the welfare bureaucracy. *Affillia, 21,* 84–96.

Labaton. S. (2007, May 25). Congress passes increase in the minimum wage. *The New York Times,* Available: http://www.nytimes.com/2007/05/25/ washington/25wage.html

Lahiri, J. (1999). *Interpreter of Maladies.* Boston: Houghton Mifflin.

Lahiri, J. (2003). *The Namesake.* Boston: Houghton Mifflin.

Lahiri, J. (2008). *Unaccustomed earth: stories.* New York: Knopf.

Landay, J. (2008, September 29). Silent racism clouds Obama's chances. *The Providence Journal,* p. C4.

Landrine, H. (1995). Introduction: Cultural diversity, contextualism, and feminist psychology. In H. Landrine (Ed.), *Bringing cultural diversity to feminist psychology,* (pp. 1–20). APA: Washington, DC.

Landrine, H., & Russo, N. (Eds.) (2010), *Handbook of feminist psychology.* New York: Springer.

Langenkamp, A. G. (2005). Latino children's integration into American society: The dynamics of bilingual education. *Sociological Focus, 38,* 115–131.

Langman, P. F. (1995). Including Jews in multiculturalism. *Journal of Multicultural Counseling & Development, 23,* 222–236.

Langston, D. (1988). Tired of playing monopoly? In J. W. Cochran, D. Langston, & C. Woodward (Eds.), *Changing our power: An introduction to women's studies* (pp. 100–110). Dubuque, IA: Kendall-Hunt.

Largely white convention frustrates black delegates. (2008, September 4). *The Providence Journal,* p. A9.

Latane, B. (1996). Dynamic social impact: The creation of culture by communication. *Journal of Communication, 46* (4), 13–25.

Leaper, C., & Ayres, M. M. (2007). A meta-analytic review of gender variations in adults' language use: Talkativeness, affiliative speech, and assertive speech. *Personality and Social Psychology Review, 11,* 328–363.

Lee, A. (1999, February 21). Black like us. *The New York Times Book Review,* p. 8.

Lee, B. A., & Marlay, M. (2007). The right side of the tracks: Affluent neighborhoods in the metropolitan United States. *Social Science Quarterly, 88,* 766–789.

Lee, C., & Owens, R. G. (2002). Issues for a psychology of men's health. *Journal of Health Psychology, 7*, 209–217.

Lee, C. C., & Rchardson, B.L. (1991). Promise and pitfalls of multicultural counseling. In C.C. Lee & B. L. Richardson (Eds.), *Multicultural issues in counseling: New approaches to diversity* (pp. 3–9). American Association for Counseling and Development: Alexandria, VA.

Lee, F. R. (2008, February 6). Inspirational African-American histories on PBS. *The Providence Journal*, p. E8.

Lehecka, R., & Delbanco, A. (2008, January 22). Ivy-league letdown. *The New York Times*. Available: http://www.nytimes.com/2008/01/22/opinion/22lehecka.html

Lehman, D. R., Chiu, C-Y, & Schaller, M. (2004). Psychology and culture. *Annual Review of Psychology, 55*, 689–714.

Leigh, I. W., & Brice, P. J. (2003). The visible and the invisible. In J. D. Robinson & L. C. James (Eds.), *Diversity in human interactions: The tapestry of America* (pp. 175–194). New York: Oxford University Press.

Leland, J. (2008, October 7). In 'sweetie' and 'dear,' a hurt for the elderly. *The New York Times,* p. A1.

Leland, J., Rhodes, S., Katel, P., Kalb, C., Peyser, M., Jospeh, N., & Brant, M. (2000). Bisexuality emerges as a new sexual identity. In P. C. R. Rust (Ed.), *Bisexuality in the United States* (pp. 560–566). New York: Columbia University Press.

Leonhardt, D. (2007, September 30). The new affirmative action. *The New York Times Magazine*, pp. 76–82.

Lev, A. I. (2007). Transgender communities: Developing identity through connection. In K. J. Bieschke, R. M. Perez, & K. A. DeBord (Eds.), *Handbook of counseling and psychotherapy with lesbian, gay, bisexual clients* (pp. 147–175). Washington, DC: American Psychological Association.

Lewin, T. (2005, May 19). Up from the holler: Living in two worlds, at home in neither. *The New York Times*. Available: http://www.nytimes.com/2005/05/19/national/class/DELLA-FINAL.html

Lewin, T. (2008, June 10). Report takes aim at 'model minority' stereotype of Asian-American students. *The New York Times*. Available: http://www.nytimes.com/2008/06/10/education/10asians.html

Liebow, E. (1967). *Tally's corner: Study of Negro streetcorner men*. Boston: Little, Brown.

Liladhar, J. (1999). Racial categories: Appearance and othering. *Feminism & Psychology, 9*, 239–242.

Little, A. G. (2007, September 2). Not in whose backyard? *The New York Times Magazine*, p. 17.

Liu, W. M. (2001). Expanding our understanding of multiculturalism: Developing a social class worldview model. In. D. B. Pope-Davis &

H. L. K. Coleman (Eds.), *The intersection of race, class, and gender in multicultural counseling* (pp. 127–170). Thousand Oaks, CA: Sage.

Liu, W. M. (2005). The study of men and masculinity as an important multicultural competency consideration. *Journal of Clinical Psychology, 61,* 685–697.

Liu, W. M., Pickett, T., Jr., & Ivey, A. (2007). White middle-class privilege: Social class bias and implications for training and practice. *Journal of Multicultural Counseling & Development, 35,* 194–206.

Locke, M. (2007, December 30). Heroes of the home front: Rosies still riveting at California National Park. *The Providence Journal,* p. A2.

Lonner, W. J. (1994). Culture and human diversity. In E. J. Trickett, R. J. Watts, & D. Birman (Eds.), *Human diversity: Perspectives on people in context* (pp. 230–243). San Francisco: Josey-Bass.

Lonner, W. J., & Hayes, S. A. (2004). Understanding the cognitive and social aspects of intercultural competence. In R. J. Sternberg & E. L. Grigorenko (Eds.), *Culture and competence: Contexts of life success* (pp. 89–110). Washington, DC: American Psychological Association.

Lott, B. (1979). Sex role ideology and children's drawings: Does the Jack-o-lantern smile or scare? *Sex Roles, 5,* 93–98.

Lott, B. (1987). Sexist discrimination as distancing behavior: I. A laboratory demonstration. *Psychology of Women Quarterly, 11,* 47–58.

Lott, B. (1994). *Women's lives: Themes and variations in gender learning* (2nd edition). Pacific Grove, CA: Brooks/Cole.

Lott, B. (1997). The personal and social correlates of a gender difference ideology. *Journal of Social Issues, 53,* 279–298.

Lott, B. (2001). Low-income parents and the public schools. *Journal of Social Issues, 57,* 247–259.

Lott, B. (2003). Violence in low-income neighborhoods in the United States: Do we care? *Journal of Aggression, Maltreatment & Trauma, 8(4),* 1–15.

Lott, B., & Bullock. H. E. (2007). *Psychology and economic injustice: Personal, professional, and political intersections.* Washington, DC: American Psychological Association.

Lott, B., & Lott, A. J. (1985). Learning theory in contemporary social psychology. In E. Aronson & G. Lindzey (Eds.), *Handbook of social psychology. Vol III* (pp. 109–135). Reading, MA: Addison-Wesley.

Lott, B., & Maluso, D. (1993). The social learning of gender. In A. E. Beall & R. J. Sternberg (Eds.), *The psychology of gender* (pp. 99–123). New York: Guilford.

Lott, B., & Saxon, S. (2002). The influence of ethnicity, social class, and context on judgments about U.S. women. *Journal of Social Psychology, 142,* 481–499.

Lui, M. (2006). *The color of wealth: The story behind the U.S. racial wealth divide.* New York: New Press.

Malcolmson, S. L. (2000). *One drop of blood: The American misadventure of race.* New York: Farrar, Straus & Giroux.

Maluso, D. (1995). Shaking hands with a clenched fist: Interpersonal racism. In B. Lott & D. Maluso (Eds.), *The social psychology of interpersonal discrimination* (pp. 50–79). New York: Guilford.

Mann, S. A., & Kelley, L. R. (1997). Standing at the crossroads of modernist thought: Collins, Smith, and the new feminist epistemologies. *Gender & Society, 11,* 391–408.

Mann, W. J. (1997). A boy's own class. In Raffo, S. (Ed.), *Queerly classed: Gay men and lesbians write about class* (pp. 217–226). Boston: South End Press.

Marcus, S. (2005). Queer theory for everyone: A review essay. *Signs, 31,* 191–218.

Markus, H. R. (2008). Pride, prejudice, and ambivalence: Toward a unified theory of race and ethnicity. *American Psychologist, 63,* 651–670.

Martin, D. (2008, May 6). Mildred Loving, who battled ban on mixed-race marriage, dies at 68. *The New York Times,* Available: http://www.nytimes.com/2008/05/06/us/06loving.html

Marx, D. M., Brown, J. L., & Steele, C. M. (1999). Alport's legacy and the situational press of stereotypes. *Journal of Social Issues, 55,* 491–502.

Matsumoto, D. (1994). *Cultural influence on research methods and statistics.* Pacific Grove, CA: Brooks/Cole.

Matsumoto, D. (Ed.). (2001). *The handbook of cultural psychology.* New York: Oxford University Press.

Maton, K. I. (2000). Making a difference: The social ecology of social transformation. *American Journal of Community Psychology, 28,* 25–57.

Mattis, J., Grayman, N., Cowie, S., Winston, C., Watson, C., & Jackson, D. (2008). Intersectional identities and the politics of altruistic care in a low-income, urban community. *Sex Roles, 59,* 418–428.

McDermott, M., & Samson, F. L. (2005). White racial and ethnic identity in the United States. *Annual Review of Sociology, 31,* 245–261.

McDowell, T., & Fang, S-R. S. (2007). Feminist-informed critical multiculturalism: Considerations for family research. *Journal of Family Issues, 28:* 549–566.

McIntosh, P. (1988). White privilege and male privilege: A personal account of coming to correspondences through work in Women's Studies. In R. Delgado & J. Stefancic (Eds.), *Critical white studies: Looking behind the mirror* (pp. 291–299). Philadelphia, PA: Temple University Press.

McLaren, P. (1999). Unthinking whiteness: Rethinking democracy: critical citizenship in gringolandia. In C. Clark & J. O'Donnell (Eds.), *Becoming and unbecoming White: Owning and disowning a racial identity.* Westport, CT: Bergin & Garvey.

Merkin, D. (2007, October 14). Money always talks. *The New York Times Magazine,* p. 110.

Miller, R. J. (2007, March 21). Cutting native peoples' health care. *Tom Paine.* Available: http://www.tompaine.com/articles/2007/03/21/cutting_native_peoples_health_care.php

Mio, J. S., Trimble, J. E., Arredondo, P., Cheatham, H. E., & Sue, D. (1999). *Key words in multicultural interventions: A dictionary.* Westport, CT: Greenwood.

Mio, J. S., Barker-Hackett, L., & Tumambing, J. (2006). *Multicultural psychology: Understanding our diverse communities.* Boston: McGraw Hill.

Mishan, L. (2008, August 3). Perseverance brings misfortune. *The New York Times Book Review,* p. 11.

Moodley, R., & Curling, D. (2006). Multiculturalism. In Y. Jackson (Ed.), *Encyclopedia of multicultural psychology* (pp. 324–325). Thousand Oaks, CA: Sage.

Moradi, B., & Rottenstein, A. (2007). Objectification theory and deaf culture identity attitudes: Roles in deaf women's eating disorder symptomology. *Journal of Counselng Psychology, 54,* 178–188.

Morales, E. (2002). *Living in Spanglish: The search for Latino identity in America.* New York: St. Martin's Press.

Moss, K. (2003). *The color of class: Poor Whites and the paradox of privilege.* Philadelphia: University of Pennsylvania Press.

Mozes, A. (2008, February 21). Poverty drains nutrition from family diet. *HealthDay Reporter.* Available: http://findarticles.com/p/articles/mi_kmhea/is_ai_n2432799

Muhammad, D. (2008, June 30). Race and extreme inequality. *The Nation,* p. 26.

Mullings, L. (1997). *On our own terms: Race, class and gender in the lives of African American women.* New York: Routledge.

Mullings, L. (2004). Domestic policy and human security in the U. S. *Peace Review, 16:1,* 55–58.

Munsey, C. (2007, June). Stereotype-busting people can spur stress, reduce cognitive performance. *Monitor on Psychology,* p. 11.

Murphy, M. C., Steele, C. M., & Gross, J. J. (2007). Signaling threat: How situational cues affect women in math, science, and engineering settings. *Psychological Science, 18,* 879–885.

Muwakkil, S. (2008, December). Proud of Obama ... For now. *In These Times,* p. 15.

Nagata, D. K. (2000). World War II internment and the relationships of Nisei women. In J. L. Chin (Ed.), *Relationships among Asian American women* (pp. 49–70). Washington, DC: American Psychological Association.

Nagel, J. (1994). Constructing ethnicity: Creating and recreating ethnic identity and culture. *Social Problems, 41*, 152–176.

Napier, J. L., & Jost, J. T. (2008). Why are conservatives happier than liberals? *Psychological Science, 19*, 565–572.

National Advisory Mental Health Council. (1996). *Sociocultural and environmental processes*. Washington, DC: National Institute of Mental Health.

National Women's History Museum. (2008). *Chinese American women, a history of resilience and resistance*. Available: http://www.nwhm.org/Chinese/1.html

Navarro, M. (2003, November 9). Going beyond Black and White, Hispanics in census pick 'other'. *The New York Times*, p. YT 1, 21.

Navarro, M. (2008, March 31). Who are we? New dialogue on mixed race. Available: http://www.nytimes.com/2008/03/31/us/politics/32race.html

Nelson, J. (2008, February 10). Identity politics. *The New York Times Book Review*, pp. 18–19.

Nelson, M. K., & Schutz, R. (2007). Day care differences and the reproduction of social class. *Journal of Contemporary Ethnography, 36*, 281–317.

Nelson. M. L., Englar-Carlson, M., Tierney, S. C., & Hau, J. M. (2006). Class jumping into academia: Multiple identities for counseling academics. *Journal of Counseling Psychology, 53*, 1–14.

Nenga, S. K. (2003). Social class and structure of feeling in women's childhood memories of clothing, food, and leisure. *Journal of Contemporary Ethnography, 32*, 167–199.

Nero, C. J. (2005). Why are the gay ghettoes White? In E. P. Johnson & M. G. Henderson (Eds.), *Black queer studies: A critical anthology* (pp. 228–245). Durham, NC: Duke University Press.

New project seeks justice for vulnerable children. (2007, winter). *SPLC Report, 37*(4).

Newcomb, T. M., Koenig, K. E., Flacks, R., & Warwick, D. P. (1967). *Persistence and change: Bennington college and its students after 25 years*. New York: Wiley.

Niemann, Y. F. (2001). Stereotypes about Chicanas and Chicanos: Implications for counseling. *Counseling Psychologist, 29*, 5–90.

Nightingale, D., & Neilands, T. (1997). Understanding and practicing critical psychology. In D. Fox & I. Prilleltensky (Eds.), *Critical psychology: An introduction* (pp. 68–84). Thousand Oaks, CA: Sage.

Nisbett, R. E. (2007, December 9). All brains are the same color. *The New York Times*, p. WK 11.

Nisbett, R. E. (2009). *Intelligence and how to get it: Why schools and culture count*. New York: W. W. Norton.

Noer, M. (2006, August 23). Point: Don't marry career women. Available: http://www.forbes.com/2006/08/23/marriage-careers-divorce_cx_mn_land.html.

Novotney, A. (2008, May). Preventing harassment at schools. *Monitor on Psychology*, 18–19.

Oates, J. C. (2007). *The gravedigger's daughter: a novel*. New York: Ecco.

Obama, B. (1995). *Dreams from my father: A story of race and inheritance*. New York: Crown.

Obama, B. (2008, March 18). Speech on race, delivered in Philadelphia. *The New York Times*. Available: www.nytimes.com/2008/03/18/us/politics/18text-obama.html

Okazaki, S., & Hall, G. C. N. (2002). Introduction: The who, what, and how of Asian American psychology. In G. C. N. Hall & S. Okazaki (Eds.), *Asian American psychology: The science of lives in context* (pp. 3–11). Washington, DC: American Psychological Association.

Oliver, W. (2006). "The streets": An alternative Black male socialization institution. *Journal of Black Studies, 36*, 918–937.

Ossorio, P., & Duster, T. (2005). Race and genetics: Controversies in biomedical, behavioral, and forensic sciences. *American Psychologist, 60*, 115–128.

Ostrove, J. M., & Cole, E. R. (2003). Privileging class: Toward a critical psychology of social class in the context of education. *Journal of Social Issues, 59*, 677–692.

Ostrove, J. M., & Long, S. M. (2007). Social class and belonging: Implications for college adjustment. *Review of Higher Education, 30*, 363–389.

Owen, D. S. (2007). Towards a critical theory of whiteness. *Philosophy & Social Criticism, 33*, 203–222.

Packard, E. (2006, March). HIV/AIDS disproportionately affects women of color, say panelists. *Monitor on Psychology*, 12.

Pastor, J., McCormick, J., Fine, M., Andolsen, R., Friedman, N., Richardson, N., Roach, T., & Tavarez, M. (2007). Makin' homes: An urban girl thing. In B. J. R. Leadbeater & N. Way (Eds.), *Urban girls revisited: Building strengths* (pp. 75–96). New York: New York University Press.

Patterson, O. (1995). The crisis of gender relations among African Americans. In A. F. Hill & E. C. Jordan (Eds.), *Race, gender, and power in America: The legacy of the Hill-Thomas hearings* (pp. 56–104). New York: Oxford University Press.

Patterson, O. (2000, October 22). America's worst idea. *The New York Times Book Review*, pp. 15–16.

Patterson, O. (2006, January 8). Being and blackness. *The New York Times Book Review*, pp. 10–11.

Payne, Y. A. (2008). "Street Life," as a site of resiliency: How street life oriented Black men frame opportunity in the United States. *Journal of Black Psychology, 34*, 3–31.

Pear, R., & Hernandez, R. (2007, February 13). States and U.S. at odds on aid for uninsured. *The New York Times*, Available: http://www.nytimes.com/2007/02/13/us/13insure.html

Pedersen, P. B. (1997). Recent trends in cultural theories. *Applied & Preventive Psychology, 6*, 221–231.

Pedersen, P. B. (Ed.). (1999). *Multiculturalism as a fourth force*. Philadelphia, PA: Bruner/Mazel.

Pelligrini, A. (1997). Whiteface performances: 'Race', gender, and Jewish bodies. In J. Boyarin & D. Boyarin (Eds.), *Jews and other differences* (pp. 108–149). Minneapolis: University of Minnesota Press.

Pennebaker, R. (2008, June 1). 'Sex' and the pink ribbon. *The New York Times*, p. WK2.

Penner, L. A., Albrecht, T. L., Coleman, D. K., & Norton, W. E. (2007). Interpersonal perspectives on Black-White health disparities: Social policy implications. *Social Issues and Policy Review, 1*, 63–98.

Pepitone, A. (2000). A social psychology perspective on the study of culture: An eye on the road to interdisciplinarianism. *Cross-cultural Research, 14*, 233–249.

Peroff, N. C., & Wildcat, D. R. (2002). Who is an American Indian? *Social Science Journal, 39*, 349–361.

Perry, P. (2001). White means never having to say you're ethnic: White youth and the construction of "cultureless" identity [Special Issue]. *Journal of Contemporary Ethnography, 30(1)*, 56–91.

Petersen, A. (2006). An African-American woman with disabilities: The intersection of gender, race, and disability. *Disability & Society, 21*, 721–734.

Phan, T. (2005). Interdependent self: Self-perception of Vietnamese-American youths. *Adolescence, 40*, 425–441.

Philaretou, A. G., & Allen, K. R. (2001). Reconstructing masculinity and sexuality. *Journal of Men's Studies, 9*, 301–321.

Phinney, J. S. (1996). When we talk about American ethnic groups, what do we mean? *American Psychologist, 51*, 918–927.

Piliavin, J. A., Grube, J. A., & Callero, P. L. (2002). Role as resource for action in public service. *Journal of Social Issues, 58*, 469–485.

Plutocracy reborn (2008, June 30). *The Nation*, 24–25.

Pogrebin, L. C. (1991). *Deborah, Golda, and me*. New York: Crown.

Pope, M. (1995). The "salad bowl" is big enough for us all: An argument for the inclusion of lesbians and gay men in any definition of multiculturalism. *Journal of Counseling & Development, 73*, 301–304.

Porter, E. (2008, November 2). Who is in the middle? *The New York Times*, p. WK9.

Prell, R. E. (1996). Terrifying tales of Jewish womanhood. In J. Rubin-Dorsky & S. F. Fishkin (Eds.), *People of the book* (pp. 98–113). Madison: University of Wisconsin Press.

Prilleltensky, I., & Fox, D. (1997). Introducing critical psychology: Values, assumptions, and the status quo. In D. Fox & I. Prilleltensky (Eds.), *Critical psychology: An introduction* (pp. 1–20). Thousand Oaks, CA: Sage.

Prilleltensky, I., & Nelson, G. (2002). *Doing psychology critically*. New York: Palgrave Macmillan.

Pugh, T. (2007, July 22). More families finding scant help. *The Providence Journal*, pp. D1,4.

Pugh-Lilly, A. (2007, Spring). Feminist motherhood column. *The Feminist Psychologist,: Newsletter of the Society for the Psychology of Women, Division of the American Psychological Association*, 95.

Purdie-Vaughns, V., & Eibach, R. P. (2008). Intersectional invisibility: The distinctive advantages and disadvantages of multiple subordinate-group identities. *Sex Roles, 59*, 377–391.

Quart, A. (2008, March 16). When girls will be boys. *The New York Times Magazine*, pp. 32–37.

Quinlan, K. J., Bowleg, L., & Ritz, S. F. (2008). Virtually invisible women: Women with disabilities in mainstream psychological theory and research. *Review of Disability Studies, 4*(*3*). 4–17.

Race is no deeper than skin, genetic scientists maintain. (1995, February 21). *The Providence Journal*, p. A6.

Race is over. (1996, September 29). *The New York Times Magazine*, pp. 170–171.

Raffo, S. (Ed.). (1997). *Queerly classed: Gay men and lesbians write about class*. Boston, MA: South End Press.

Raines, J., & McAdams, C. B. (2006, Spring). College and social class: The broken promise of America. *Crosscurrents*, 46–57.

Raj, R. (2007). Transactivism as therapy: A client self-empowerment model linking personal and social agency. In J. M. Glassgold & J. Drescher (Eds.), *Activism and LGBT psychology* (pp. 77–98). Binghampton, NY: Haworth.

Ramos-Zayas, A. Y. (2001). Racializing the "invisible" race: Latino constructions of "White culture" and whiteness in Chicago. *Urban Anthropology, 30*, 341–380.

Rappaport, J., & Stewart, E. (1997). A critical look at critical psychology: Elaborating the questions. In D. Fox & I. Prilleltensky (Eds.), *Critical psychology: An introduction* (pp. 301–317). Thousand Oaks, CA: Sage.

Ray, W. (2001). *The logic of culture*. Malden, MA: Blackwell.

Reich, R. R. (2008, February 13). Totally spent. *The New York Times*. Available: http://www.nytimes.com/2008/02/13/opinion/13reich.html

Reid, P. T. (1994). The real problem in the study of culture. *American Psychologist, 49*, 524–525.

Reid, P. T. (2002). Multicultural psychology: Bringing together gender and ethnicity. *Cultural Diversity & Ethnic Minority Psychology, 8*, 103–114.

Reid, P. T., & Comas-Diaz, L. (1990). Gender and ethnicity: Perspectives on dual status. *Sex Roles, 22*, 397–408.

Reid, P. T., Cooper, S. M., & Banks, K. H. (2008). Girls to women: Developmental theory, research, and issues. In F. L. Denmark & M. A. Paludi, (Eds.), *Psychology of women: A handbook of issues and theories* (2nd edition, 237–270). Westport, CT: Praeger.

Reis, H. T. (2008). Reinvigorating the concept of situation in social psychology. *Personality & Social Psychology Review, 12,* 311–329.

Reitman, M. (2006). Uncovering the White place: Whitewashing at work. *Social & Cultural Geography, 7,* 267–282.

Reynolds, A. L., & Pope, R. L. (1991). The complexities of diversity: Exploring multiple oppressions. *Journal of Counseling & Development, 70,* 174–180.

Reynolds, J., & Wetherell, M. (2003). The discursive climate of singleness: The consequences for women's negotiation of a single identity. *Feminism & Psychology, 13,* 489–510.

Reynolds, J., Wetherell, M., & Taylor, S. (2007). Choice and chance: Negotiating agency in narratives of singleness. *Sociological Review, 55,* 331–351.

Rhem, J. (2007, September). Social class and student learning. *Class Action,* E-news. Available: info@classism.org.

Rich, A. (1980). Compulsory heterosexuality and lesbian existence. *Signs: Journal of Women in Culture & Society, 5,* 631–660.

Riddle, B. (2007). Out of bounds: Demanding recognition for a queer identity. *Psychoanalysis, Culture & Society, 12,* 26–31.

Riggs, D. W. (2008). 'The blighted germs of heterosexual tendencies': Reading Freud in (be)hindsight. *Journal of Community & Applied Social Psychology, 18,* 131–139.

Ritz, S. F. (2003). *The stigma of poverty: The nature and implications of everyday classis.* Unpublished master's thesis. University of Tennessee at Chatanooga TN.

Ritz, S. F. (2008). *Coping with everyday classism: Experiences of low-income people in a southeastern rural community.* Unpublished doctoral dissertation. University of Rhode Island, Kingston, RI.

Rivera-Ramos, A. N. (1992). The psychological experience of Puerto Rican women at work. In S. B. Krause, P. Rosenfeld, & A. L. Culbertson (Eds.), *Hispanics in the workplace* (pp. 194–207). Newbury Park, CA: Sage.

Roan, S. (2008, August 31). Enough to make you sick. *Providence Journal,* pp. J 1,4.

Roberts, S. (2007, August 9). Minorities now form majority in one-third of most populous counties. *The New York Times.* Available: http://www. nytimes.com/2007/08/09/us/09census.html

Roberts, S. (2008a, May 1). Rise in minorities is led by children, census finds. *The New York Times.* Available: http://www.nytimes.com/2008/05/01/washington/01census.html

Roberts. S. (2008b, August 7). Minorities often a majority of the population under 20. *The New York Times*. Available: http://www.nytimes.com/2008/08/07/us/07census.html

Roccas, S., & Brewer, M. B. (2002). Social identity complexity. *Personality & Social Psychology Review, 6,* 88–106.

Rogoff, B. (2003).*The cultural nature of human development*. New York: Oxford University Press.

Root, M. P. P. (1990). Resolving "other" status: Identity development of biracial individuals. In L. S. Brown & M. P. P. Root (Eds.), *Complexity and diversity in feminist theory and therapy* (pp. 185–205). New York: Haworth.

Root, M. P. P (Ed.). (1996). *The multiracial experience.* Thousand Oaks, CA: Sage.

Root, M. P. P. (2001). Negotiating the margins. In J. G. Ponterotto, J. M. Casas, L. A. Suzuki, & C. M. Alexander (Eds.), *Handbook of multicultural counseling* (2nd edition, pp. 113–122). Thousand Oaks, CA: Sage.

Ross, M., Xun, W. Q. E., & Wilson, A. E. (2002). Language and the bicultural self. *Personality & Social Psychology Bulletin, 28,* 1040–1050.

Roylance, F. D. (2004, October 11). "A sort of scientific malpractice": Genetics: Scientists are cautioning doctors against the use of race as guide to diagnosis, treatment and research. *The Baltimore Sun,* p. 1A.

Russell, S. T. (2002). Queer in America: Citizenship for sexual minority youth. *Applied Developmental Science, 6,* 258–263.

Rust, P. C. R. (2000). The biology, psychology, sociology, and sexuality of bisexuality. In P. C. R. Rust (Ed.), *Bisexuality in the United States* (pp. 403–470). New York: Columbia University Press.

Ryan, J. L., & Sackrey, C. (1996). *Strangers in paradise: Academics from the working class.* Lanham, MD: University Press of America.

Sachs, S. (2001, March 11). Redefining minority. *The New York Times,* pp. WK 1,4.

Sack, K. (1997, February 8). Symbols of old South feed a new bitterness. *The New York Times,* p. WK1, 8.

Saletan, W. (2007, November 18). Race, genes, and intelligence. *Slate.* Available: http://www.slate.com/id/2178122/entry2178123/

Sampson, E. (1985), The decentralization of identity: Toward a revised concept of personal and social order. *American Psychologist, 40,* 1203–1211.

Sampson, E. (1989). The challenge of social change for psychology: Globalization and psychology's theory of the person. *American Psychologist, 44,* 914–921.

Satyanarayana, M. (2008, May 5). Researchers say poverty yardstick is too outdated. *The Providence Journal,* p. A5.

Sawhill, I., & Morton, J. E. (2007). *Economic mobility: Is the American dream alive and well?* Economic Mobility Project. Available: EMP American Dream Report.pdf

Schachter, E. P. (2005). Context and identity formation: A theoretical analysis and a case study. *Journal of Adolescent Research, 20,* 375–395.

Scheer, J. (1994). Culture and disability: An anthropological point of view. In E. J. Trickett, R. J. Watts, & O. Birman (Eds.), *Human diversity* (pp. 244–260). San Francisco: Jossey-Bass.

Schemo, D. J. (2006, October 21). Turmoil at college for deaf reflects broader debate. *The New York Times.* Available: http://www.nytimes/com/2006/10/21/education/21gallaudet.html

Schmid, R. E. (1999, January 20). Dropping race in cancer study urged. Available: *Microsoft Outlook Express 4.72.2106.4.*

Schneider, S. W. (1984). *Jewish and female: Choices and changes in our lives today.* New York: Simon & Schuster.

Schulman, K, & Blank, H. (2008, September). State child care assistance policies 2008: Too little progress for children and families. *National Women's Law Center Issue Brief.* Available: State Child Care Assistance Policies Report08.pdf

Schwartz, S. H., & Bardi, A. (2001). Value hierarchies across cultures: Taking a similarities approach. *Journal of Cross-Cultural Psychology, 32,* 268–290.

Seelye, K. Q., & Bosman, J. (2008, June 13). Media and critics split over sexism in Clinton coverage. *The New York Times.* Available: http://www.nytimes/com/2008/06/13/us/politics/13women.html

Segall, M. H., Lonner, W. J., & Berry, J. W. (1998). Cross-cultural psychology as a scholarly discipline: On the flowering of culture in behavioral research. *American Psychologist, 53,* 1101–1110.

Seligman, M. E. P., & Csikszentmihalyi, M. (2001). Reply to comments. *American Psychologist, 56,* 89–90.

Sen, A. (2006). *Identity and violence: The illusions of destiny.* New York: Norton.

Shelton, J. N., & Sellers, R. M. (2000). Situational stability and variability in African American racial identity. *Journal of Black Psychology, 26,* 27–50.

Sherman, A., Greenstein, R., & Parrott, S. (2008, August 26). Poverty and share of Americans without health insurance were higher in 2007 – and median income for working age households was lower – than at bottom of last recession. *Center on Budget and Policy Priorities,* Available: 8-26-08pov.pdf

Shields, S. A. (2008). Gender: An intersectionality perspective. *Sex Roles, 59,* 301–311.

Shorter-Gooden, K. (2004). Multiple resistance strategies: How African American women cope with racism and sexism. *Journal of Black Psychology, 30,* 406–425.

Shweder, R. A. (1990). Cultural psychology: What is it? In J. W. Stigler, R. A. Shweder, & G. Herdt (Eds.), *Cultural psychology: Essays on comparative human development* (pp. 1–43). Cambridge, UK: Cambridge University Press.

Sicotte, D., & Swanson, S. (2007). Whose risk in Philadelphia? Proximity to unequally hazardous industrial facilities. *Social Science Quarterly, 88,* 515–534.

Siegel, R. J., & Cole, E. (Eds.). (1997). *Celebrating the lives of Jewish women: Patterns in a feminist sampler.* New York: Harrington Park Press.

Silverstein, C. (2007). Wearing two hats: The psychologist as activist and therapist. In J. M. Glassgold & J. Drescher (Eds.), *Activism and LGBT psychology* (pp. 9–35). Binghampton, NY: Haworth.

Singletary, M. (2008, February 10). King's dream deferred, one more victim of the subprime mortgage crisis. *The Washington Post,* Available: http://classism.org/article2.php

Sklar, H. (2007, October 21). Billionaires up, America down. *Daily Camera.* Available: http://dailycamera.com/news/2007/oct/21/billionaires-ip-america-down/

Smedley, A., & Smedley, B. D. (2005). Race as biology is fiction, racism as a social problem is real. *American Psychologist, 60,* 16–26.

Smiler, A. P. (2004). Thirty years after the discovery of gender: Psychological concepts and measures of masculinity. *Sex Roles, 50,* 15–26.

Smith, E. J. (1991). Ethnic identity development: Toward the development of a theory within the context of majority/minority status. *Journal of Counseling & Development, 70,* 181–188.

Spelke, E. S. (2005). Sex differences in intrinsic aptitude for mathematics and science? *American Psychologist, 60,* 950–958.

Stanley, A. (2008). Mars and Venus dissect the Spitzer scandal on the TV talk shows. *The New York Times.* Available: http://www.nytimes.com/2008/03/12/arts/television/12watc.html

Staples, B. (2002a, April 21). The Seminole tribe, running from history. *The New York Times,* p. 12 WK.

Staples, B. (2002b, July 1). Monticello as the all-American melting pot. *The New York Times.* Available: http://www.nytimes.com/2002/07/01/opinion/01MON3.html

Staples, B. (2005, October 31). Why race isn't as 'black' and 'white' as we think. *The New York Times.* Available: http://www.nytimes.com/2005/10/31/opinion/31mon4.html.

Staples, B. (2008a, May 14). Loving v. Virginia and the secret history of race. *The New York Times.* Available: http://www.nytimes.com/2008/05/14/opinion/14wed4.html

Staples, B. (2008b, September 22). Barack Obama, John McCain and the language of race. *The New York Times.* Available: http://www.nytimes.com/2008/09/22/opinion/22observer.html

Steele, C. M. (1997). A threat in the air: How stereotypes shape intellectual identity and performance. *American Psychologist, 52,* 613–629.

Steele, C. M., & Aonson, J. (1998). Stereotype threat and the test performance of academically successful African Amricans. In C. Jencks & M. Phillips (Eds.), *The Black-White test score gap* (pp. 401–427). Washington, DC: Brookings Institution.

Stewart, A. J., & McDermott, C. (2004). Gender in psychology. *Annual Review of Psychology, 55,* 519–544.

Stewart, A. J., & Ostrove, J. M. (1993). Social class, social change, and gender: Working-class women at Radcliffe and after. *Psychology of Women Quarterly, 17,* 475–497.

Struch, N., Schwartz, S. H., & van der Kloot, W. A. (2002). Meanings of basic values for women and men: A cross-cultural analysis. *Personality & Social Psychology Bulletin, 28,* 16–28.

Stuber, J. M. (2006). Talk of class: The discursive repertoires of White work- and upper-middle-class college students. *Journal of Contemporary Ethnography, 35,* 285–318.

Sue, D. W., Bingham, R. P., Porche-Burke, L., & Vasquez, M. (1999). The diversification of psychology: A multicultural revolution. *American Psychologist, 54,* 1061–1069.

Sue, D. W., Capodilupo, C. M., Torino, G. C., Bucceri, J. M., Holden, A. M. B., Nadal, K. L., & Esquilin, M. (2007). Racial microaggressions in everyday life. *American Psychologist, 62,* 271–286.

Sue, D. W., Carter, R. T., Casaa, J. M., Fouad, N. A., Ivey, A. E., Jensen, M., et al. (1998). *Multicultural counseling competencies.* Thousand Oaks, CA: Sage.

Sue, D. W., & Sue, S. (2003). *Counseling the culturally diverse* (4th ed.) New York: Wiley.

Sue, S. (1991). Ethnicity and culture in psychological research and practice. In J. Goodchilds (Ed.), *Psychological perspectives on human diversity in America* (pp. 51–85). Washington, DC: American Psychological Association.

Sue, S. (1994). Introduction. In E. I. Trickett, R. J. Watts, & D. Birman (Eds.), *Human diversity: Perspectives on people in context* (pp. 1–4). San Francisco: Josey-Bass.

Sue, S., & Wagner, N. (Eds.). (1973). *Asian-Americans: Psychological perspectives.* Ben Lomond, CA: Science & Behavior Books.

Sullivan, E. (2008, November 15). Threats against Obama on the rise. *AOL News.* Available: http://news.aol.com/main/obama-presidency/article/threats-against-obama-on-the-rise/249016

Sun, K. (1995). The definition of race. *American Psychologist, 50,* 43–44.

Suresha, R. J. (2005). Introduction. In R. J. Suresha & P. Chvany (Eds.), Bi-men: Coming out every which way (pp. 3–9). New York: Haworth.

Swarns, R. L. (2008, August 25). Blacks debate civil rights risk in Obama's rise. *The New York Times.* Available: http://www.nytimes.com/2008/08/25/us/politics/25racw.html

Swartz, M. J. (2001). On the substance and uses of culture's elements. *Cross Cultural Research, 35* (*2*), 179–200.

Szulc, T. (1999, January 3). The fastest growing minority in America. *Parade,* pp. 4–7.

Tagliabue, J. (2007, October 2). For the yachting class, the latest amenity can take flight. *The New York Times,* Available: http://www.nytimes.com/2007/10/02/business/02yacht.html

Talley, A. E., & Bettencourt, B. A. (2007). Evaluations and aggression directed at a gay male target: The role of threat and antigay prejudice. *Journal of Applied Social Psychology, 36,* 647–683.

Tan, A. (1989). *The Joy Luck Club.* New York: Putnam.

Tan, A. (2001). *The bonesetter's daughter.* New York: Putnam.

Tan, A. (2006). *The kitchen god's wife.* New York: Penguin.

Tavris, C. (1991). The mismeasure of woman: Paradoxes and perspectives in the study of gender. In J. D. Goodchilds (Ed.), *Psychological perspectives on human diversity in America* (pp. 87–136). Washington, DC: American Psychological Association.

Taylor, J. K. (2007). Transgender identities and public policy in the United States: The relevance for public administration. *Administration & Society, 39,* 833–856.

Tebes, J. K. (2000). External validity and scientific psychology. *American Psychologist, 55,* 1508–1509.

The cold war threat to the Navajo. (2008, February 12). *The New York Times.* Available: http://www.nytimes.com/2008/02/12/opinion/12tue3.html

The new face of race. (2000, September 18). *Newsweek,* 38–41.

Thomas, V. G. (2004). The psychology of Black women: Studying women's lives in context. *Journal of Black Psychology, 30,* 286–306.

Tien, L. (2000). U.S. attitudes toward women of Asian ancestry: Legislative and media perspectives. In L. Chin (Ed.), *Relationships among Asian American women* (pp. 29–47). Washington, DC: American Psychological Association.

Tierney, J. (2008, September 9). As barriers disappear, some gender gaps widen. *The New York Times, p.,* F1.

Tomasello, M. (2001). Cultural transmission: A view from chimpanzees and human infants. *Journal of Cross-Cultural Psychology, 32,* 135–146.

Tough, P. (2007, June 10). The class-consciousness raiser. *The New York Times Magazine,* pp. 52–56.

Traub, J. (2007, October 14). The measures of wealth. *The New York Times Magazine,* pp. 21–22.

Trimberger, E. K. (2005). *The new single woman.* Boston: Beacon Press.

Tsai, J. L., Chentsova-Dutton, Y., & Wong, Y. (2002). Why and how researchers should study ethnic identity, acculturation, and cultural orientation. In C. C. N. Hall & S. Okazaki (Eds.), *Asian American psychology:*

The science of lives in context (pp. 41–65). Washington, DC: American Psychological Association.

Uchitelle, L. (2008, July 22). Women are now equal as victims of poor economy. *The New York Times.* Available: http://www.nytimes.com/2008/07/22/business/22jobs.html

Unger, R. K. (1979). Toward a redefinition of sex and gender. *American Psychologist, 34,* 1085–1094.

University of Maryland, Asian American Studies Program (2008). *A Portrait of Chinese Americans.* Available: http://www.aast.umd.edu

Urbina, I. (2008, August 27). A decline in uninsured is reported for 2007. *The New York Times,* Available: http://www.nytimes.com/2008/08/27/washington/27census.html

Vanderbosch, J. (1997). Notes from the working class. In S. Raffo (Ed.), *Queerly classed: Gay men and lesbians write about class* (pp. 83–94). Boston, MA: South End Press.

Vandore, E., Keller, G. (2008, October 22). Income gap widens in wealthiest nations. *San Francisco Chronicle,* A13.

Vasquez, C. (1997). Spirit and passion. In S. Raffo (Ed.), *Queerly classed: Gay men and lesbians write about class* (pp. 121–134). Boston: South End Press.

Vaughan, D. (2002). Signals and interpretive work: The role of culture in a theory of practical action. In K. Cerulo (Ed.), *Culture in minds: Toward a sociology of culture and cognition* (pp. 28–54). New York: Routledge.

Vedantam, S. (2008, March 24). Unequal perspectives on racial equality. *Washington Post,* p. A3.

Wade, N. (2008, September 16). A dissenting voice as the genome is sifted to fight disease. *The New York Times.* Available: http://www.nytimes.com/2008/09/16/science/16prof.html

Waldman, P. (2007, December 5). *Workers are paying the price for our productivity-focused, growth-at-any-cost business world. Why aren't the candidates talking about it?* Available: http:www.prospect.org/cs/articles?article=woe-is-the-american-worker

Wallace, B. (2006). Cross cultural psychology. In Y. Jackson (Ed.), *Encyclopedia of multicultural psychology* (pp. 115–121). Thousand Oaks, CA: Sage.

Wang, V. O., & Sue, S. (2005). In the eye of the storm: Race and genomics in research and practice. *American Psychologist, 60,* 37–45.

Warner, L. R. (2008). A best practices guide to intersectional approaches in psychological research. *Sex Roles, 59,* 454–463.

Washington, L. S. (2008, December). Obama needs a Black agenda. *In These Times,* p. 17.

Wasserman. D. (2008, March 16). Cartoon. *The New York Times,* p. WK.

Watters, E. (2007, August 12). Suffering differently. *The New York Times Magazine,* p. 15.

Weber, L. (1998). A conceptual framework for understanding race, class, gender, and sexuality. *Psychology of Women Quarterly, 22,* 13–32.

Weeks, M., & Lupfer, M. B. (2004). Complicating race: Relationships between prejudice, race, and social class categorizations. *Personality & Social Psychology Bulletin, 30,* 972–984.

Weller, C. (2008, January/February). The erosion of middle class economic security after 2001. *Challenge, 51,* 45–68.

Wellman, D. (1999). Transforming received categories: Discovering cross-border identities and other subversive activities. In C. Clark & J. O'Donnell (Eds.), *Becoming and unbecoming White: Owning and disowning a racial identity* (pp. 78–91). Westport, CT: Greenwood.

West, C. (1993). *Prophetic reflections: Notes on race and power in America.* Monroe, ME: Common Courage Press.

West, C., & Fenstermaker, S. (1996). Doing difference. In E. N-L. Chow, D. Wilkinson, & M. B. Zinn (Eds.), *Race, class and gender: Common bonds, different voices* (pp. 357–384). Thousand Oaks, CA: Sage.

What's white, anyway? (2000, September 18). *Newsweek,* pp. 64–65.

Whitman, J. S., Horn, S.S., & Boyd, C. J. (2007). Activism in the schools: Providing LGBTQ affirmative training to school counselors. In J. M. Glassgold & J. Drescher (Eds.), *Activism and LGBT psychology* (pp. 9–35). Binghampton, NY: Haworth.

Williams, M. (1999, March 7). Is there a Black upper class? *The New York Times,* pp. ST 1,2.

Williams, T., & Correal, A. (2008, May 30). Sex and the rest of the city. *The New York Times.* Available: www.nytimes.com/2008/05/30/nyregion/30reax/html

Willis, D. J., Bigfoot, D. S. (2003). On native soil: The forgotten race: American Indian. In J. D. Robinson & L. C. James (Eds.), *Diversity in human interactions: The tapestry of America* (pp. 77–91). New York: Oxford University Press.

Willow, M. G. (1997). Class struggles. In Raffo, S. (Ed.) (1997). *Queerly classed: Gay men and lesbians write about class* (pp. 105–117). Boston: South End Press.

Wilson, R. (2009). Puncturing the genome myth: Why the genetic code fails to explain gendered behavior. In J. W. White (Ed.) *Taking sides: Clashing views on gender* (4th edition) (pp. 9–12). Boston: McGraw-Hill.

Wilson, W. J. (1998). The role of the environment in the Black-White test score gap. In C. Jencks & M. Phillips (Eds.) *The Black-White test score gap* (pp. 501–510). Washington, DC: Brookings Institution.

Wingrove, W. (1999). Interpellating sex. *Signs, 24,* 869–893.

Worchel, S. (1999). *Written in blood: Ethnic identity and the struggle for human harmony.* New York: Worth.

Working Families e-Activist Network, AFL-CIO. (2006, May 16) *Tell McDonalds and Chipotle to support fair wages for farm workers.* Available: http://www.unionvoice.org

Ybarra, M. A. (2003). Becoming Americano. In J. D. Robinson & L. C. James (Eds.), *Diversity in human interactions: The tapestry of America* (pp. 21–31). New York: Oxford University Press.

Yee, A. H., Fairchild, H. H., Wizman, E., & Wyatt, G. E. (1993). Addressing psychology's problems with race. *American Psychologist, 48,* 1132–1140.

Yee, A. H. (2006, March/April). Is psychology's race albatross nearing its end? *The National Psychologist,* 12.

Your Money. (2008, March). Job prospects? *AARP Bulletin,* 14.

Yu, T. (2006). Challenging the politics of the "model minority" stereotype: A case for educational equality. *Equity & Excellence in Education, 39,* 325–333.

Zipperer, B., & Schmitt, J. (2008, January 25). Union rates increase in 2007. *Truthout.* Available: http://www.truthout.org/issues_06/printer_012508_A_shtml

Zucker, A. N., & Ostrove, J. M. (2007). Meanings of sex and gender for a new generation of feminist psychologists. *Feminism & Psychology, 17,* 470–474.

Zuckerman, A. (2008, March 7). Pew report and the American Jewish community. *Jewish Voice & Herald,* p. 5.

Zuckerman, M. (1990). Some dubious premises in research and theory on racial differences. *American Psychologist. 45,* 1287–1303.

Zweig, M. (2008, March 31). The war and the working class. *The Nation,* pp. 20–26.

Name Index

Note: academic writers are listed by surname plus initial(s); others by surname plus full given name

Subject Index